The Official Rails-to-Trails Conservancy Guidebook

T0247435

Rail-Trails
Minnesota

The definitive guide to the state's top multiuse trails

 WILDERNESS PRESS . . . *on the trail since 1967*

Rail-Trails: Minnesota

Copyright © 2016 by Rails-to-Trails Conservancy
First edition, fifth printing 2024

Maps: Lohnes+Wright; Map data courtesy of Environmental Systems Research Institute
Cover design: Scott McGrew
Book design: Annie Long

Library of Congress Cataloging-in-Publication Data
 Names: Rails-to-Trails Conservancy, issuing body.
 Title: The official Rails-to-Trails Conservancy guidebook. Rail-trails Minnesota.
 Other titles: Rail-trails Minnesota
 Description: Birmingham, AL : Wilderness Press, 2016. | Includes index.
 Identifiers: LCCN 2015050749 | ISBN 9780899978215
 Subjects: LCSH: Rail-trails—Minnesota—Guidebooks. | Outdoor recreation—
  Minnesota—Guidebooks. | Minnesota—Guidebooks
 Classification: LCC GV191.42.M6 O44 2016 | DDC 796.509776—dc23
 LC record available at http://lccn.loc.gov/2015050749

Manufactured in China

Published by:  WILDERNESS PRESS
 An imprint of AdventureKEEN
 2204 First Ave. S, Ste. 102
 Birmingham, AL 35233
 800-678-7006; fax 877-374-9016
 info@wildernesspress.com
 wildernesspress.com

Visit wildernesspress.com for a complete listing of our books and for ordering information. Contact us at our website, at facebook.com/wildernesspress1967, or at twitter
.com/wilderness1967 with questions or comments. To find out more about who we are
and what we're doing, visit our blog, blog.wildernesspress.com.

Distributed by Publishers Group West

Front cover: Mesabi Trail (see page 101); photographed by Paul Stafford © Explore Minnesota. *Back cover:* Dinkytown Greenway (see page 50); photographed by Tom Watson.

SAFETY NOTICE: Although Wilderness Press and Rails-to-Trails Conservancy have
made every attempt to ensure that the information in this book is accurate at press time,
they are not responsible for any loss, damage, injury, or inconvenience that may occur to
anyone while using this book. You are responsible for your own safety and health while in
the wilderness. The fact that a trail is described in this book does not mean that it will be
safe for you. Be aware that trail conditions can change from day to day. Always check local
conditions, know your own limitations, and consult a map.

About Rails-to-Trails Conservancy

Headquartered in Washington, D.C., Rails-to-Trails Conservancy (RTC) is a nonprofit organization dedicated to creating a nationwide network of trails from former rail lines and connecting corridors to build healthier places for healthier people.

Railways helped build America. Spanning from coast to coast, these ribbons of steel linked people, communities, and enterprises, spurring commerce and forging a single nation that bridges a continent. But in recent decades, many of these routes have fallen into disuse, severing communal ties that helped bind Americans together.

When RTC opened its doors in 1986, the rail-trail movement was in its infancy. While there were some 250 known miles of open rail-trails in the United States, most projects focused on single, linear routes in rural areas, created for recreation and conservation. RTC sought broader protection for the unused corridors, incorporating rural, suburban, and urban routes.

Year after year, RTC's efforts to protect and align public funding with trail building created an environment that allowed trail advocates in communities across the country to initiate trail projects. These ever-growing ranks of trail professionals, volunteers, and RTC supporters have built momentum for the national rail-trails movement. As the number of supporters multiplied, so did the rail-trails.

Americans now enjoy more than 22,000 miles of open rail-trails, and as they flock to the trails to connect with family members and friends, enjoy nature, and get to places in their local neighborhoods and beyond, their economic prosperity, health, and overall well-being continue to flourish.

A signature endeavor of RTC is **TrailLink.com,** America's portal to these rail-trails, as well as other multiuse trails. When RTC launched **TrailLink.com** in 2000, our organization was one of the first to compile such detailed trail information on a national scale. Today, the website continues to play a critical role in both encouraging and satisfying the country's growing need for opportunities to ride, walk, skate, or run for recreation or transportation. This free trail-finder database—which includes detailed descriptions, interactive maps, photo galleries, and first-hand ratings and reviews—can be used as a companion resource to the trails in this guidebook.

The national voice for more than 160,000 members and supporters, RTC is committed to ensuring a better future for America made possible by trails and the connections they inspire. Learn more at **railstotrails.org.**

West River Parkway Trail is part of the Grand Rounds National Scenic Byway, a 50-plus-mile network of trails that circles Minneapolis (see page 146).

Table of Contents

About Rails-to-Trails Conservancy iii

Foreword vii

Acknowledgments ix

Introduction 1

How to Use This Book 3

1 Afton to Lakeland Trail 8

2 Beaver Island Trail 11

3 Big Rivers Regional Trail 14

4 Blazing Star State Trail 17

5 Bottineau Trail 20

6 Brown's Creek State Trail 23

7 Bruce Vento Regional Trail 26

8 Cannon Valley Trail 29

9 Casey Jones State Trail 32

10 Cedar Lake LRT Regional Trail 35

11 Central Lakes State Trail 38

12 Cuyuna Lakes State Trail 41

13 Dairyland Trail 44

14 Dakota Rail Regional Trail 47

15 Dinkytown Greenway .50

16 Douglas State Trail 53

17 Gateway State Trail 56

18 Gitchi-Gami State Trail 59

19 Glacial Lakes State Trail 62

20 Goodhue Pioneer State Trail 65

21 Great Northern Trail 68

22 Great River Ridge State Trail 71

23 Greenway of Greater Grand Forks 74

24 Hardwood Creek Regional Trail 77

25 Harmony-Preston Valley State Trail 80

26 Heartland State Trail .83

27 Hiawatha Trail. 86

28 Interstate State Park to Taylors Falls Trail. 89

29 Lake Minnetonka LRT Regional Trail. 92

30 Lake Wobegon Trail. 95

31 Luce Line Trail. 98

32 Mesabi Trail 101

33 Midtown Greenway. 104

34 Minnehaha Trail. 107

35 Minnesota Valley State Trail 110

36 Mississippi River Regional Trail (Dakota County) . . . 113

37 North Cedar Lake Regional Trail 116

38 Paul Bunyan State Trail. 119

39 Red Jacket Trail 122

40 Rocori Trail 125

41 Root River State Trail 128

42 Sakatah Singing Hills State Trail. 131

43 Shooting Star State Trail 134

44 St. Anthony Falls Heritage Trail 137

45 Sunrise Prairie Trail. 140

46 Western Waterfront Trail. 143

47 West River Parkway Trail. 146

48 Willard Munger State Trail 149

Index 154

Photo Credits 162

Support Rails-to-Trails Conservancy 163

Foreword

For those of you who have already experienced the sheer enjoyment and freedom of riding on a rail-trail, welcome back! You'll find *Rail-Trails: Minnesota* to be a useful and fun guide to your favorite trails, as well as an introduction to pathways you have yet to travel.

For readers who are discovering for the first time the adventures possible on a rail-trail, thank you for joining the rail-trail movement. Since 1986, Rails-to-Trails Conservancy has been the leading supporter and defender of these priceless public corridors. We are excited to bring you *Rail-Trails: Minnesota,* so you, too, can enjoy some of this state's rail-trails and multiuse trails. These hiking and biking trails are ideal ways to connect with your community, with nature, and with your friends and family.

I've found that trails have a way of bringing people together, and as you'll see from this book, you have opportunities in every city you visit to get on a great trail. Whether you're looking for a place to exercise, explore, commute, or play, there is a trail in this book for you.

So I invite you to sit back, relax, pick a trail that piques your interest—and then get out, get active, and have some fun. I'll be out on the trails too, so be sure to wave as you go by.

Happy trails,
Keith Laughlin, President
Rails-to-Trails Conservancy

The Great River Ridge State Trail passes by this grain cooperative that began in 1908 (see page 71).

Acknowledgments

Many thanks to the following contributors and to all the trail managers we called on for assistance to ensure the maps, photographs, and trail descriptions are as accurate as possible:

Cindy Dickerson

Amy Kapp

Jake Laughlin

Kesi Marcus

Maggie Morris

Jon Rayer

Laura Stark

Elizabeth Striano

Tom Watson

Long stretches of the Root River State Trail are shaded by a canopy of trees (see page 128).

Introduction

Of the more than 1,900 rail-trails across the United States, 70 are located in the state of Minnesota, known for one of the best developed and diverse trail networks in the country and second among states in total rail trail mileage. Built on unused, former railroad corridors, these trails tread storied routes of westward expansion and industrialization and offer a glimpse into life a century ago. Today they bear the signature of their history: tunnels, trestles, raised berms, and depots in communities born and abandoned.

Minnesota, once the center of railway activity in the country, is credited for supplying much of the ore from the Mesabi Iron Range to the steel industry that produced the planes, ships, and tanks that led to victory in World War II. Rail-trails retrace the tracks of these railways, as well as those of other passenger and freight lines. Their original purposes and destinations vary, but each of these rail-trails joins past with present, creating a living memorial of the corridors that helped shape the region.

We are delighted to bring you a selection of 48 trails that represent some of the best rail-trails and greenways in the state. These trails traverse Minnesota's diverse topography including extensive prairies, lakes, rivers, parks, and woodlands linking urban and rural communities and providing a multitude of options to explore the best of Minnesota. Our selection includes the 123-mile Paul Bunyan State Trail, one of the longest rail-trails in the United States featuring spectacular scenery as it passes by more than 20 lakes, rivers, and streams with abundant wildlife and quaint small towns along the way. Not to be missed is the Red Jacket Trail featuring a restored depot and three converted railroad trestles including the stunning 80-foot-high Red Jacket Trestle over the Le Sueur River. Minneapolis's famed Stone Arch Bridge is the highlight on the St. Anthony Falls Heritage Trail, which offers a short 1.8-mile loop showcasing the bridge's 23 arches made from native granite and limestone and the best view of the falls below.

No matter which route in *Rail-Trails: Minnesota* you decide to try, you'll be touching on the heart of the community that helped build it and the history that first brought the rails to the region.

What Is a Rail-Trail?

Rail-trails are multiuse public paths built along former railroad corridors. Most often flat or following a gentle grade, they are suited to walking, running, cycling, mountain biking, in-line skating, cross-country skiing, horseback riding, and wheelchair use. Since the 1960s, Americans have created more than 22,000 miles of rail-trails throughout the country.

These extremely popular recreation and transportation corridors traverse urban, suburban, and rural landscapes. Many preserve historical landmarks, while others serve as wildlife conservation corridors, linking isolated parks and establishing greenways in developed areas. Rail-trails also stimulate local economies by boosting tourism and promoting trailside businesses.

What Is a Rail-with-Trail?

A rail-with-trail is a public path that parallels a still-active rail line. Some run adjacent to high-speed, scheduled trains, often linking public transportation stations, while others follow tourist routes and slow-moving excursion trains. Many share an easement, separated from the rails by extensive fencing. More than 250 rails-with-trails exist in the United States.

Both cyclists and pedestrians yield to deer on the Lake Wobegon Trail (see page 95).

How to Use This Book

Rail-Trails: Minnesota provides the information you'll need to plan a rewarding trail trek. With words to inspire you and maps to chart your path, it makes choosing the best route a breeze. Following are some of the highlights.

Maps

You'll find two levels of maps in this book: a **state locator map** and **detailed trail maps.**

Use the state locator map to find the trails nearest to you, or select several neighboring trails and plan a weekend hiking or biking excursion. Once you find a trail on the state locator map, simply flip to that trail's detail page for a full description. Accompanying trail maps mark each route's access roads, trailheads, parking areas, restrooms, and other defining features.

Key to Map Icons

Parking

Drinking water

Restrooms

Trail Descriptions

Trails are listed in alphabetical order. Each description leads off with a set of summary information, including trail endpoints and mileage, a roughness index, the trail surface, and possible uses.

The map and summary information list the trail endpoints (either a city, street, or more specific location) with suggested points from which to start and finish. Additional access points are marked on the maps and mentioned in the trail descriptions. The maps and descriptions also highlight available amenities, including parking and restrooms, as well as such area attractions as services, museums, parks, and stadiums. Trail length is listed in miles.

Each trail bears a **roughness index** rating from 1 to 3. A rating of 1 indicates a smooth, level surface that is accessible to users of all ages and abilities. A 2 rating means the surface may be loose and/or uneven and could pose a problem for road bikes and wheelchairs. A 3 rating suggests a rough surface that is recommended only for mountain bikers and hikers. Surfaces can range from asphalt or concrete to ballast, boardwalk, cinder, crushed stone, gravel, grass, dirt, sand, and/or wood chips. Where relevant, trail descriptions address alternating surface conditions.

All trails are open to pedestrians, and most allow bicycles, except where noted in the trail summary or description. The summary also indicates wheelchair access. Other possible uses include in-line skating, mountain biking, hiking, horseback riding, fishing, and cross-country skiing. While most trails are off-limits to motor vehicles, some local trail organizations do allow all-terrain vehicles (ATVs) and snowmobiles.

Trail descriptions themselves suggest an ideal itinerary for each route, including the best parking areas and access points, where to begin, your direction of travel, and any highlights along the way. Following each description are directions to the recommended trailheads.

Each trail description also lists a local website for further information. Be sure to visit these websites in advance for updates and current conditions. **TrailLink.com** is another great resource for updated content on the trails in this guidebook.

Trail Use

Rail-trails are popular destinations for a range of users, often making them busy places to enjoy the outdoors. Following basic trail etiquette and safety guidelines will make your experience more pleasant.

Keep to the right, except when passing.

Pass on the left, and give a clear audible warning: "Passing on your left."

Be aware of other trail users, particularly around corners and blind spots, and be especially careful when entering a trail, changing direction, or passing, so that you don't collide with traffic.

Respect wildlife and public and private property; leave no trace and take out litter.

Control your speed, especially near pedestrians, playgrounds, and heavily congested areas.

Travel single file. Cyclists and pedestrians should ride or walk single file in congested areas or areas with reduced visibility.

Cross carefully at intersections; always look both ways and yield to through traffic. Pedestrians have the right-of-way.

Keep one ear open and volume low on portable listening devices to increase your awareness of your surroundings.

Wear a helmet and other safety gear if you're cycling or in-line skating.

Consider visibility. Wear reflective clothing, use bicycle lights, or bring flashlights or helmet-mounted lights for tunnel passages or twilight excursions.

Keep moving, and don't block the trail. When taking a rest, turn off the trail to the right. Groups should avoid congregating on or blocking the trails. If you have an accident on the trail, move to the right as soon as possible.

Bicyclists yield to all other trail users. Pedestrians yield to horses. If in doubt, yield to all other trail users.

Dogs are permitted on most trails, but some trails through parks, wildlife refuges, or other sensitive areas may not allow pets; it's best to check the trail website before your visit. If pets are permitted, keep your dog on a short leash and under your control at all times. Remove dog waste in a designated trash receptacle.

Teach your children these trail essentials, and be especially diligent to keep them out of faster-moving trail traffic.

Be prepared, especially on long-distance rural trails. Bring water, snacks, maps, a light source, matches, and other equipment you may need. Because some areas may not have good reception for mobile phones, know where you're going, and tell someone else your plan.

Key to Trail Use

cycling

in-line skating

fishing

wheelchair access

horseback riding

mountain biking

snowmobiling

walking

cross-country skiing

Learn More

To learn about additional rail-trails in your area or to plan a trip to an area beyond the scope of this book, visit Rails-to-Trails Conservancy's trail-finder website, **TrailLink.com,** a free resource with information on more than 30,000 miles of trails nationwide.

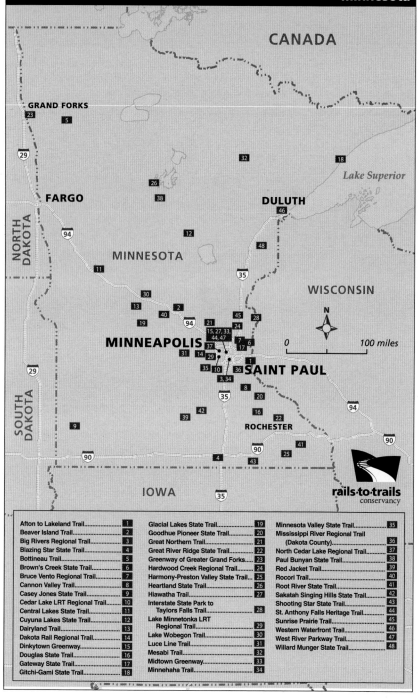

Minnesota

CANADA

GRAND FORKS

FARGO

NORTH DAKOTA

MINNESOTA

DULUTH

Lake Superior

WISCONSIN

MINNEAPOLIS

SAINT PAUL

SOUTH DAKOTA

ROCHESTER

IOWA

N

0   100 miles

rails·to·trails
conservancy

Afton to Lakeland Trail	1
Beaver Island Trail	2
Big Rivers Regional Trail	3
Blazing Star State Trail	4
Bottineau Trail	5
Brown's Creek State Trail	6
Bruce Vento Regional Trail	7
Cannon Valley Trail	8
Casey Jones State Trail	9
Cedar Lake LRT Regional Trail	10
Central Lakes State Trail	11
Cuyuna Lakes State Trail	12
Dairyland Trail	13
Dakota Rail Regional Trail	14
Dinkytown Greenway	15
Douglas State Trail	16
Gateway State Trail	17
Gitchi-Gami State Trail	18
Glacial Lakes State Trail	19
Goodhue Pioneer State Trail	20
Great Northern Trail	21
Great River Ridge State Trail	22
Greenway of Greater Grand Forks	23
Hardwood Creek Regional Trail	24
Harmony-Preston Valley State Trail	25
Heartland State Trail	26
Hiawatha Trail	27
Interstate State Park to Taylors Falls Trail	28
Lake Minnetonka LRT Regional Trail	29
Lake Wobegon Trail	30
Luce Line Trail	31
Mesabi Trail	32
Midtown Greenway	33
Minnehaha Trail	34
Minnesota Valley State Trail	35
Mississippi River Regional Trail (Dakota County)	36
North Cedar Lake Regional Trail	37
Paul Bunyan State Trail	38
Red Jacket Trail	39
Rocori Trail	40
Root River State Trail	41
Sakatah Singing Hills State Trail	42
Shooting Star State Trail	43
St. Anthony Falls Heritage Trail	44
Sunrise Prairie Trail	45
Western Waterfront Trail	46
West River Parkway Trail	47
Willard Munger State Trail	48

Minnesota

A restored railroad bridge crosses the Clearwater River on the Bottineau Trail (see page 20).

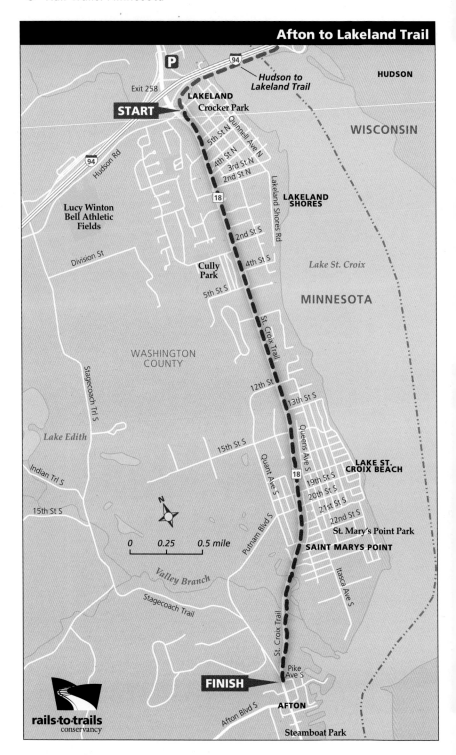

Afton to Lakeland Trail

HUDSON

Exit 258

P

94

Hudson to Lakeland Trail

94

Hudson Rd

LAKELAND

START

Crocker Park

WISCONSIN

5th St N

Quinnell Ave N

4th St N

3rd St N

2nd St N

18

LAKELAND SHORES

Lakeland Shores Rd

Lucy Winton Bell Athletic Fields

2nd St S

Division St

Cully Park

4th St S

Lake St. Croix

5th St S

MINNESOTA

WASHINGTON COUNTY

St. Croix Trail

Stagecoach Trl S

12th St

13th St S

Lake Edith

15th St S

Queens Ave S

Quant Ave S

Indian Trl S

18

19th St S

LAKE ST. CROIX BEACH

15th St S

20th St S

21st St S

22nd St S

St. Mary's Point Park

N

Putnam Blvd S

SAINT MARYS POINT

0   0.25   0.5 mile

Itasca Ave S

Valley Branch

Stagecoach Trail

St. Croix Trail

Pike Ave S

FINISH

rails·to·trails
conservancy

AFTON

Afton Blvd S

Steamboat Park

The Afton to Lakeland Trail links its namesake towns on the Minnesota side of the St. Croix River. The trail runs between Quinlan Avenue North/Eighth Street at Crocker Park in Lakeland and Pike Avenue South near Afton City Hall (the southern trailhead). The flat trail passes through Lakeland Shores, Lake St. Croix, Lake St. Croix Beach, and Saint Marys Point.

Although this trail travels through the lower portion of the beautiful St. Croix River Valley, it runs parallel to the highway (St. Croix Trail South/County Road 18) for its entire length, with the closest view of the river 0.25 mile to the east.

The northern trailhead is linked to the Hudson to Lakeland/Afton Trail that crosses over the St. Croix River via the I-94 pedestrian bridge/bikeway and travels immediately north into the town of Hudson, Wisconsin. Though

Although largely urban, the trail takes on a woodsy, rural feel toward Afton.

Location
Washington

Endpoints
Hudson Road N./Eighth St. N. and Quinlan Ave. N. (Lakeland) to Pike Ave. S. and St. Croix Trail S. (Afton)

Mileage
4

Type
Rail-Trail

Roughness Index
1

Surface
Asphalt

the trail in Lakeland begins its run through five semi-urban river communities along a relatively busy highway, the landscape becomes more woodsy and inviting along its southern segment toward Afton. The section that crosses Valley Branch Creek is on a railroad grade through a floodplain and includes tree-covered hills.

Beyond the southern trailhead at Afton City Hall, trail users can continue south into the old village section of Afton via city streets and a pathway between 32nd and 34th Streets. Restrooms and supplies need to be sought out in the communities along the route, although there is a portable toilet at the city park in the old village section of Afton.

CONTACT: metrobiketrails.weebly.com/washington-county.html

DIRECTIONS

To reach the southern trailhead from I-94, take Exit 258. Head 5 miles south on St. Croix Trail/ County Road 18. Turn left onto Pike Ave. S. Limited parking is available at Afton City Hall.

To reach the northern trailhead, from I-94, take Exit 258. Head south on St. Croix Trail/ CR 18, and immediately turn left onto Hudson Road N./Eighth St. N., and access the trail at the intersection with Quinlan Ave. N. in Lakeland.

You can also access the trail at its midpoint on Fourth St. and park at Afton-Lakeland Elementary School on weekends, or park farther south of the school off Seventh St. To reach this trail access, from I-94, take Exit 258. Head 1.3 miles south on St. Croix Trail/CR 18, and turn left just past Fourth St. into the school parking lot. To reach Seventh St., head 1.5 miles south on St. Croix Trail from the interstate.

Beaver Island Trail follows the route of an inactive railway that was originally part of a charter railroad of the Minneapolis and Northwestern Railway Company. Built in 1882, the railroad line connected Minneapolis with the town of Clearwater, south of St. Cloud. A spur line connects to Tileston, a site where a mill and elevator were located adjacent to a dam on the Mississippi River.

Today the Beaver Island Trail, once known as the Tileston Mill Spur, is open in two disconnected segments. The larger segment follows the Mississippi River for a little more than 5 miles from near the St. Cloud State University campus south to Montrose Road at Clearwater Road. North of the university campus, a short segment is available behind the St. Cloud River's Edge Convention Center.

The Beaver Island Trail follows a route near the Mississippi River and St. Cloud State University.

Location
Stearns

Endpoints
First St. N. to Second St. S. along the west side of the Mississippi River and University Drive S. at First Ave. S. to Montrose Road and Clearwater Road (St. Cloud)

Mileage
6.1

Type
Rail-Trail

Roughness Index
1

Surface
Asphalt

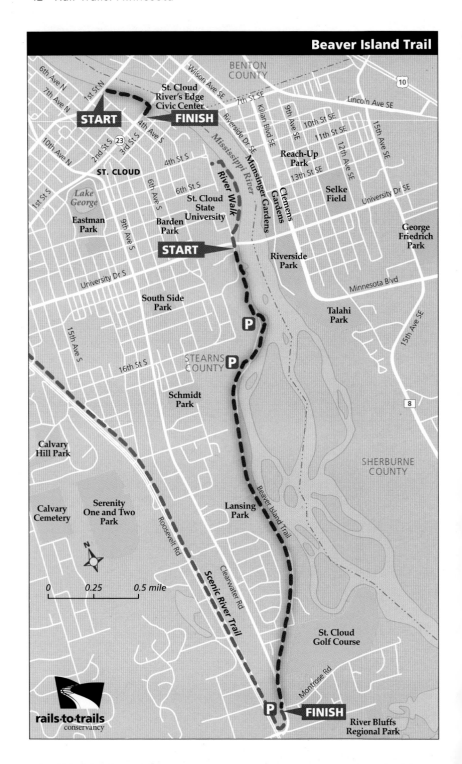

Beaver Island Trail

At 33rd Street South and Roosevelt Road/County Road 75, the Beaver Island Trail links up to the Scenic River Trail, which is neither scenic nor along the river, but does provide a direct, nondescript route back north into downtown at McKinley Park at 10th Street South.

Beyond the northern terminus of the larger segment of the Beaver Island Trail on First Avenue South is the River Walk, a predominantly pedestrian trail that follows along the river as it skirts about five blocks of downtown streets.

CONTACT: co.stearns.mn.us/recreation/trailsandconditions/bikewaysand
bikingtrails

DIRECTIONS

To reach the southern terminus of the trail near River Bluffs Regional Park from I-94, take Exit 171 for County Road 75/Roosevelt Road. Head 0.8 mile north on Roosevelt Road. Turn right onto 38th St. S. Parking will be on the left.

Additional access points for the trail are at the St. Cloud State University campus, beyond the east end of 15th St. and 16th St. on Third Ave. S. (there is a bicycle tune-up station here), and at 33rd St. S. and CR 75/Roosevelt Road.

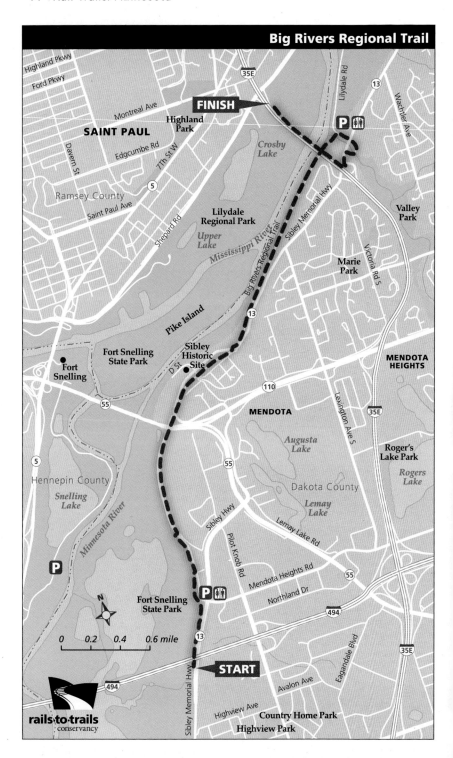

Big Rivers Regional Trail

Highland Pkwy
Ford Pkwy
Montreal Ave
SAINT PAUL
Highland Park
Edgcumbe Rd
7Th St W
Davern St
FINISH
35E
Lilydale Rd
13
Wachtler Ave

Crosby Lake

Ramsey County
Saint Paul Ave
5
Shepard Rd

Lilydale Regional Park
Upper Lake
Mississippi River
Big Rivers Regional Trail
Sibley Memorial Hwy

P

Valley Park

Marie Park
Victoria Rd S

Pike Island

13

Fort Snelling State Park
Sibley Historic Site
D St

Fort Snelling

55

110

MENDOTA HEIGHTS

MENDOTA

35E

5
Hennepin County
Snelling Lake

Minnesota River

Augusta Lake

55

Lexington Ave S

Dakota County
Lemay Lake
Lemay Lake Rd

Roger's Lake Park
Rogers Lake

Sibley Hwy
Pilot Knob Rd

55

P

Fort Snelling State Park

Mendota Heights Rd
Northland Dr

494

35E

13

0   0.2   0.4   0.6 mile

N

Sibley Memorial Hwy

START

494

Avalon Ave

Eagandale Blvd

rails·to·trails
conservancy

Highview Ave
Country Home Park
Highview Park

The Big Rivers Regional Trail runs along the upper portion of what was originally a two-tiered section of railroad track built for one of the state's oldest lines, the Minnesota Central Railroad. At several points along its 4.4 paved miles, trail users will enjoy some of the best views overlooking the convergence of the Minnesota and Mississippi Rivers. Vistas include broad views of both river basins and glimpses of Minnesota's first military outpost and National Historic Landmark, Fort Snelling, situated just beyond Pike Island at the confluence of the two rivers. As the trail approaches its northern end near the Pool & Yacht Club in Lilydale, the view upriver toward downtown Saint Paul is equally impressive.

In the city of Mendota (one of Minnesota's oldest settlements), the trail skirts through residential areas on a raised railroad bed, crossing D Street for easy access, and

Saint Paul's skyline comes into view from the confluence of the Minnesota and Mississippi Rivers.

Location
Dakota

Endpoints
I-494 at Sibley Memorial Hwy./MN 13 (Mendota Heights) to I-35E at Shepard Road (Saint Paul)

Mileage
4.4

Type
Rail-Trail

Roughness Index
1

Surface
Asphalt

lies only one block from Sibley Memorial Highway/MN 13, which runs through the center of the city. Following D Street a few blocks past the highway and beyond the Sibley Historic Site leads to the start of the Snelling State Park Bottomlands Trail, a rough-terrain route best suited for serious mountain bikers.

The trail is accessible from several points along its route, including MN 55 in Mendota Heights, I-494 0.5 mile west of Pilot Knob Road in Eagan, and I-35E in Mendota Heights.

The Big Rivers Regional Trail is part of the extensive 72-mile Mississippi National River and Recreation Area, itself part of an even greater network consisting of hundreds of miles of trails throughout the Twin Cities area.

CONTACT: www.co.dakota.mn.us/parks/parkstrails/bigrivers

DIRECTIONS

To access the Big Rivers Regional Trail in Mendota Heights, from the I-35E and I-494 interchange in Saint Paul, take I-494 W. to Exit 71. Turn right (north) onto Pilot Knob Road, and go 0.2 mile. Turn left onto Mendota Heights Road, and go 0.3 mile to the parking lot at the stone overlook.

A smaller parking lot is available at the north end of the trail just off MN 13, at the bottom of the hill on Lilydale Road, at the railroad trestle next to the Pool & Yacht Club. From I-35E N., take Exit 102. Head northeast on MN 13, and immediately turn right onto Lilydale Road. In 0.2 mile see the parking lot on your left.

The Blazing Star State Trail is located in Albert Lea, near Minnesota's southern border. The town is known as "The Land Between the Lakes," and the trail begins on the northern shore of one of the state's larger bodies of water, Albert Lea Lake.

You can begin your journey in Frank Hall Park, which offers restrooms, picnic areas, and water. At Garfield Avenue/East Front Street, there is a parking lot where the trail also becomes the northern segment of a 0.75-mile double loop; this loop gives users an option to circle around a marshy area on the north shore of the lake before continuing on toward Myre–Big Island State Park.

The trail continues through the east side of the city before entering the rural landscapes to the state park, a scenic natural gem of wetlands, oak savanna, Big Woods, and prairie. Spring and fall bird migrations make this one of Minnesota's premier bird-watching parks.

The smooth, 6-mile paved trail is popular in the winter season for cross-country skiing.

Location
Freeborn

Endpoints
Frank Ave. and James Ave. to the railroad bridge over Albert Lea Lake in Myre–Big Island State Park (Albert Lea)

Mileage
6

Type
Rail-with-Trail

Roughness Index
1

Surface
Asphalt (unpaved 0.5-mile section in the park)

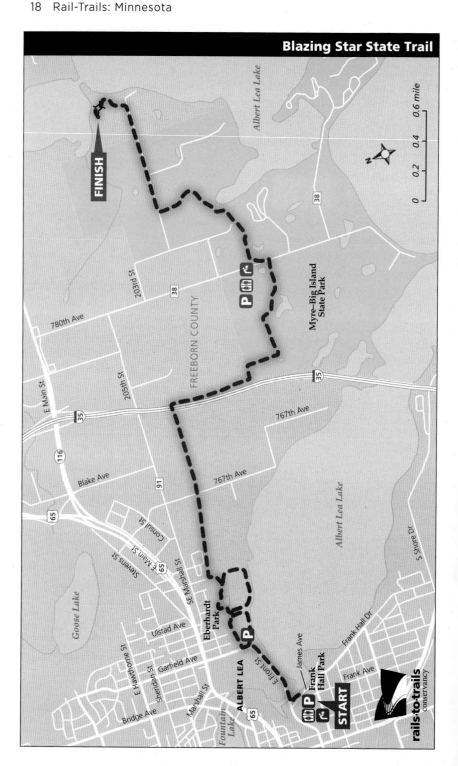

Blazing Star State Trail

The current pathway is nearly 6 miles long and paved for all but a 0.5-mile section in the park, just before the bridge at the eastern trailhead. Future plans call for extending it about 14 miles east to Austin's trail network and the Shooting Star State Trail. The initial extension, currently under construction, will take the trail from the eastern trailhead in the park, over an inactive Canadian Pacific Railroad bridge across Albert Lea Lake, and to the small town of Hayward, which is 1.5 miles to the east. A long-term goal is to extend the trail from Albert Lea all the way east to the Mississippi River.

CONTACT: dnr.state.mn.us/state_trails/blazingstar

DIRECTIONS

Two parking areas are available at the west end of the trail. The first is adjacent to Frank Hall Park at the intersection of Frank Ave. and James Ave. From the I-90/I-35 interchange in Albert Lea, head south on I-95, and take Exit 12. Continue on US 65 S. 1.8 miles. Turn left onto Garfield Ave., which becomes E. Front St. One lot will be on your left in 0.2 mile. To reach the other lot, go 0.8 mile on Garfield Ave./E. Front St., and turn left onto Frank Ave. Turn left onto James Ave., and parking will be on your left.

Parking can also be found in Myre–Big Island State Park. From I-35, take Exit 11. Head east on County Road 46/E. Main St., and go 0.6 mile. Turn right onto CR 38/780th Ave., and travel south 1.5 miles to the main entrance of the park and a parking lot near the trail.

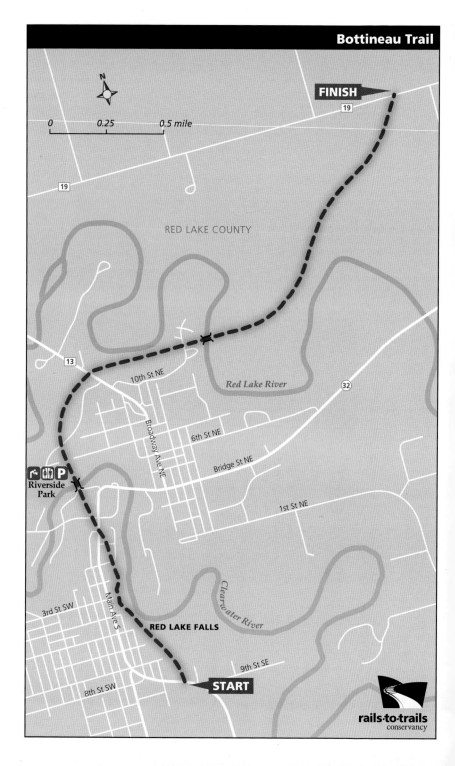

Bottineau Trail

FINISH

19

N

0   0.25   0.5 mile

19

RED LAKE COUNTY

13

10th St NE

Red Lake River

32

Broadway Ave NE

6th St NE

Bridge St NE

Riverside
Park

1st St NE

3rd St SW

Main Ave S

Clearwater River

RED LAKE FALLS

9th St SE

8th St SW

START

rails·to·trails
conservancy

The 3-mile-long Bottineau Trail runs through the small town of Red Lake Falls to a rural area to its north. The trail is named after Pierre Bottineau, a Minnesota frontiersman who died in the community in 1895. Scenery along the rail-trail includes a mix of residences and industrial properties within the city limits. Once you cross the Red Lake River, however, the northern half of the route runs through dense forest. The experience is highlighted by crossings over both the beautiful Red Lake and Clearwater Rivers on restored railroad bridges.

From the south end, the first mile of this short trail weaves through the neighborhoods of Red Lake Falls and through the center of town, offering easy street access to shops along the city portion of the trail.

If you access the trail from Riverside Park, about 1 mile north of the southern end of the trail, you will find

Looking east from a railroad bridge crossing, you can see the Clearwater River.

Location
Red Lake

Endpoints
MN 32 near Dow Ave. S.E. to County Road 19, 0.6 mile west of MN 32 (Red Lake Falls)

Mileage
3

Type
Rail-Trail

Roughness Index
1

Surface
Asphalt

restrooms, water, a picnic area, and camping. Access between the trail and the park is via a short spur that links up with the southern end of the railroad bridge in the residential section.

From this trail junction, you can head north across the historic, 467-foot-long Warren pony truss bridge, built in 1915, and over the Clearwater River; you'll continue for about 0.5 mile before crossing County Road 13.

The trail continues on another 0.5 mile through a wooded corridor to where it crosses the Red Lake River, a popular put-in site for local river tubers. The Bottineau Trail ends about 1 mile ahead at its northern terminus at CR 19. Because there is no parking at this end, this is a good turnaround point for an out-and-back round-trip from the park along the most scenic and historic segment of this short trail.

CONTACT: redlakefalls.com/index.php/community/arts-culture

DIRECTIONS

From I-29, take Exit 141 for US 2 in Grand Forks, ND. Follow US 2/Gateway Drive 6.5 miles east, and turn left onto County Road 17. Head east 22.7 miles into Minnesota. Continue straight on CR 13, and go 13.1 miles to Red Lake Falls. Turn right onto Bridge St. N.E., and in 0.3 mile continue on Main Ave. In 0.1 mile turn right onto Bottineau Ave. N.W., and park at Riverside Park on the right. The park is about 1 mile north of the southern end of the trail. Parking can also be found along city streets closer to the southern trailhead.

The 5.9-mile Brown's Creek State Trail, which opened in October 2014, is the latest addition to Minnesota's extensive trail system. The rail-trail stretches from the St. Croix riverfront town of Stillwater to meet up with the popular Gateway State Trail in the town of Grant, thus becoming part of the expansive Willard Munger State Trail system. With this connection, trail users have direct access to the St. Croix River via off-road trails from the capital city of Saint Paul to Stillwater.

The paved route follows the former Minnesota Zephyr line that operated a dinner train along the route until 2008. Noted for its scenery, the route passes through woodlands along a 2-mile stretch of dedicated trout stream and through a mile-long corridor alongside the St. Croix River, a National Scenic Riverway and Minnesota's only river in the National Wild and Scenic Rivers System.

Enjoy the autumn colors as you travel through Minnesota's noted scenic woodlands.

Location
Washington

Endpoints
Laurel St. E. and MN 95/
St. Croix Trail at the St.
Croix River (Stillwater)
to Gateway State Trail
at MN 96 and Dellwood
Road N. (Grant)

Mileage
5.9

Type
Rail-Trail

Roughness Index
1

Surface
Asphalt

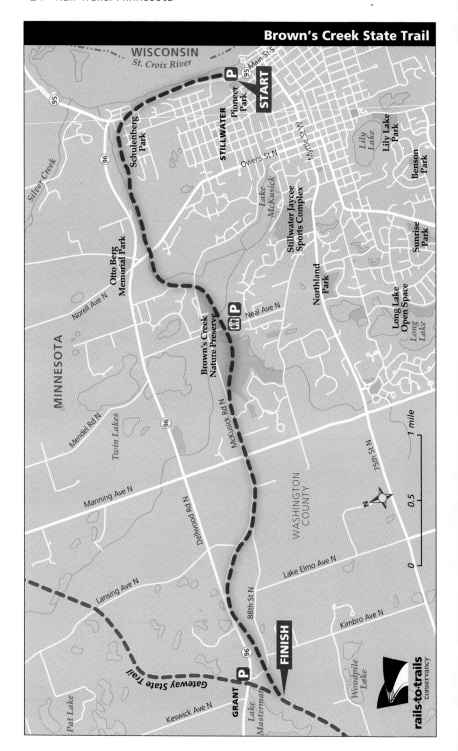

The trail passes several historic sites. It also enables users to connect to local and regional parks and trails in the Stillwater area.

The Minnesota Department of Natural Resources has installed a bicycle tune-up station in downtown Stillwater, two blocks south of the trail near Water Street. A second station is proposed for the Brown's Creek Nature Preserve, located about halfway along the trail west of Stillwater.

Restrooms are located 0.25 mile south of the eastern trailhead at the pedestrian walkway, and seasonally at the Brown's Creek Nature Preserve on Neal Avenue, halfway along the trail on the left. A seasonal portable toilet is also located on the Gateway State Trail at MN 96, 0.25 mile northeast of the intersection with the Brown's Creek State Trail.

CONTACT: dnr.state.mn.us/state_trails/browns_creek

DIRECTIONS

To access the trail in Stillwater, from Saint Paul, take I-694 to Exit 52B. Merge onto MN 36 E., and go 8.5 miles. Turn left onto MN 95 N./St. Croix Trail. In 2 miles, parking will be on the left at Laurel St.

Midway on the trail, parking is available at Brown's Creek Nature Preserve. From Saint Paul, take I-694 to Exit 52B. Merge onto MN 36 E., and go 5 miles. Turn left onto Manning Ave. N., and go 2.6 miles. Turn right onto McKusick Road N., and in 1 mile, turn right onto Neal Ave. N. Parking will be on the right in 0.1 mile.

To access the trail in Grant, from Saint Paul, take I-694 to Exit 52B. Merge onto MN 36 E., and go 0.5 mile. Take the exit toward Hilton Trail, and follow Hilton north 1.5 miles. Turn right onto Stillwater Road/75th St. N., and go 1.2 miles. Turn left onto Jamaca Ave. In 1.9 miles, turn right onto MN 96/Dellwood Road. Parking will be on the right near the trestle bridge at 1.4 miles. Follow the Gateway State Trail southwest 0.25 mile to reach Brown's Creek State Trail.

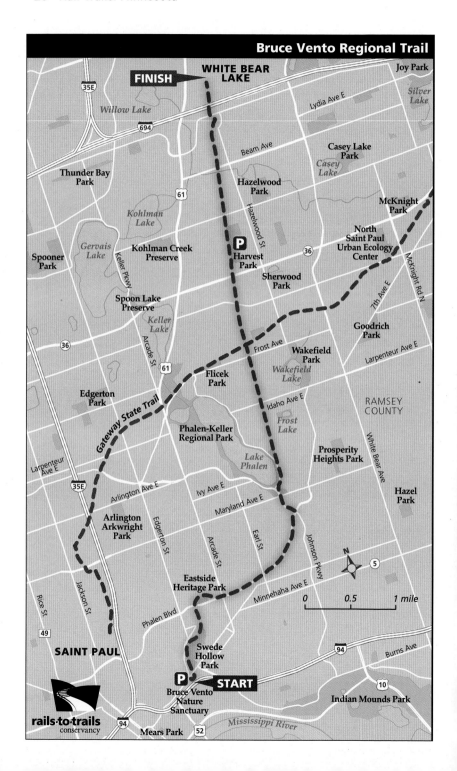

Bruce Vento Regional Trail

The trail is named in honor of Bruce Frank Vento, a member of the U.S. House of Representatives from 1977 until his death in 2000, representing Minnesota's fourth congressional district. Vento is recognized for his efforts to clean up the environment.

The regional trail links the White Bear Lake area with the Bruce Vento Nature Sanctuary on the eastern edge of downtown Saint Paul, near the Mississippi River. From the nature sanctuary, the trail heads north and immediately passes through the stone arches of the bridge known as the Seventh Street Improvement Arches. Built in 1884, it is considered one of the most important feats of engineering in Minnesota history and one of the few examples of this style of construction in the United States—not to mention the only one of its type in Minnesota. Locally quarried limestone was used for most of the stonework: The wing

The route winds through a metropolitan corridor of trees and residential areas.

Location
Ramsey

Endpoints
Bruce Vento Nature Sanctuary at Seventh St. E. and Payne Ave. (Saint Paul) to Buerkle Road, 0.2 mile east of US 61 (Vadnais Heights)

Mileage
7.5

Type
Rail-Trail

Roughness Index
1

Surface
Asphalt

walls and abutments were carved from Saint Paul gray limestone, and buff-colored Kasota limestone came from quarries in the Minnesota River Valley.

The trail then meanders northward within the scenic ravine that cuts through Swede Hollow Park, passing an industrial area before circling around and through Eastside Heritage Park. From this point northward, the trail continues through a decidedly urban setting. The route follows close to the east side of Lake Phalen, but instead of staying right along the lake on East Shore Drive, it veers away from the lake along a tree-lined corridor. For an open, direct view of the lake, trail users can jump on the Lake Phalen trail and reconnect with the Vento Trail by turning east on Arlington Avenue and accessing the trail at North English Street. From there, you'll wind through a wooded corridor between neighborhood backyards as you make your way toward White Bear Lake.

About 0.75 mile south of MN 36, the trail intersects with the Gateway State Trail, whose northeast segment continues on to its trailhead north of Stillwater. While this section is predominantly residential, the Vento Trail does pass through a few neighborhood parks and open spaces as it gets farther north.

The trail drops down along the street soon after crossing Beam Avenue at County Road D, where it then winds along the sidewalk for a short distance before resuming along a corridor that ends unglamorously at Buerkle Road, just north of I-694.

CONTACT: parks.co.ramsey.mn.us/parks/pages/trails.aspx

DIRECTIONS

For access to the southern trailhead, take I-94 to Exit 243 for Mounds Blvd. Head north on Mounds Blvd., and take the first left onto Seventh St. E. The parking lot for the Bruce Vento Nature Sanctuary is one block west, on the south side of the street at Payne Ave.

The trail can also be accessed at most road crossings. Parking is available midway along the trail at Harvest Park. From Saint Paul, follow I-35E N. to Exit 111A. Merge onto MN 36 E. toward Stillwater, and go 1.9 miles. Exit onto US 61 N., and go 0.7 mile. Turn right onto County Road C E., and in 0.8 mile turn right onto Hazelwood St. In 0.3 mile turn right onto Brooks Ave. E., and go 0.1 mile to arrive at Harvest Park. The trail is on the west end of the park.

There is no designated north trailhead at Buerkle Road.

The trail links the southeast Minnesota communities of Red Wing, Welch, and Cannon Falls along a path that follows the former route of the Chicago Great Western Railway line that once ran through this river valley. In addition to offering stunning views of the Cannon River, the trail meanders under lush canopies of hardwoods, along steep slopes with exposed rock ridges, and along bucolic country roads.

The cities of Cannon Falls and Red Wing and Goodhue County have jointly managed the trail since 1986. Although the trail has a drop of 115 feet between the cities at each end, the rail-turned-trail slope is gradual throughout its route, which winds through a striking mix of wetlands, river bluffs, several large lakes, and rolling farmland.

The trail was dedicated on May 31, 1986, with the towns of Cannon Falls and Red Wing, in addition to Goodhue County, agreeing to jointly manage the trail. The

The path connects three communities and offers stunning views of the Cannon River Valley.

Location
Goodhue

Endpoints
Archie Swenson Softball Fields on Cannon River Ave., near Almond St. N. (Cannon Falls), to Old W. Main St. and Bench St. north of US 61 (Red Wing)

Mileage
19.7

Type
Rail-Trail

Roughness Index
1

Surface
Asphalt

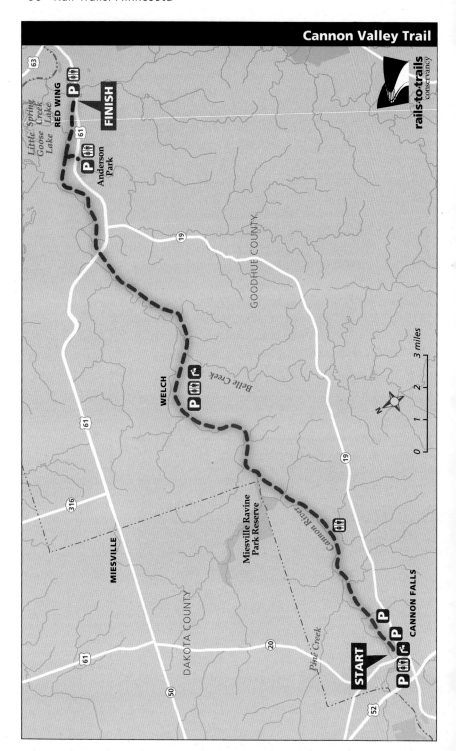

Cannon Valley Trail

rails-to-trails
conservancy

RED WING

Little Spring
Goose Creek
Lake   Lake

P

FINISH

Anderson
Park

P

GOODHUE COUNTY

WELCH

Belle Creek

P

MIESVILLE

Miesville Ravine
Park Reserve

Cannon River

DAKOTA COUNTY

Prairie Creek

CANNON FALLS

P

P

START

N

0   1   2   3 miles

former Chicago Great Western corridor actually extends westward even farther to the city of Mankato. Between that city and Faribault, the Sakatah Singing Hills State Trail is open on the former rail line for recreational use. The planned Mill Towns Trail will fill the gap on the corridor between Faribault and Cannon Falls; when completed, trail users will be able to travel from Red Wing to Mankato on nearly 100 miles of uninterrupted rail-trails.

To help pay for maintenance of the Cannon Valley Trail, trail users age 18 and older require a Wheel Pass when using the trail April 1–November 1. Passes can be purchased at kiosks at major access points to the trail and at local businesses; pedestrians and wheelchair users are exempt. In Red Wing, a city trail beginning several blocks east of the trailhead will take you south for about 2 miles to the northern trailhead of the Goodhue Pioneer State Trail.

Using the Welch Station trailhead as the midpoint-loop starting point, the 7-mile sections provide an out-and-back option west toward Cannon Falls and east to Anderson Park in Red Wing. These sections are among the most scenic of the valley and also avoid most urban development at each end.

Restrooms are available in Cannon Falls, Anderson Memorial Rest Area, Welch Station, Old West Main Street access, and Bay Point Park in Red Wing.

CONTACT: cannonvalleytrail.com

DIRECTIONS

To begin in Cannon Falls, from I-35, take Exit 76. Head east on County Road 2/Deuce Road, and go 0.8 mile. Turn right onto CR 46/Pillsbury Ave., and go 1.8 miles. Turn left onto CR 86/280th St. E., and go 16.8 miles. Make a slight left onto Rochester Blvd., and cross US 52. Go 2.6 miles, as the road changes to CR 29 and then MN 20. Turn left onto Dakota St. W., and take the first right onto N. Third St. In 0.2 mile, after crossing Cannon River, turn left onto Water St. In 0.1 mile turn left onto Stoughton St. E. and then onto Cannon River Ave. After 0.5 mile, turn right to go behind the city wastewater treatment facility to the city softball fields. Parking will be on the left.

To reach the trailhead in Welch, from I-35, take Exit 86. Head east on 162nd St. W./CR 46, and go 19.6 miles. Continue straight on CR 47/Vermillion Road 2.1 miles. Turn right onto Vermillion St., and in 0.4 mile, turn left onto MN 316 S./Red Wing Blvd. Go 9.8 miles. Turn left onto US 61 S. and go 2 miles. Turn right onto County 7 Blvd., and go 2.7 miles. Turn right onto Mt. Hill Road and go 0.1 mile. Turn left into the parking area.

To reach the eastern trailhead in Red Wing, take I-494 to Exit 63B. Continue straight on Hastings Blvd. S./US 61, and go 2.4 miles. Turn left onto MN 316 S./Red Wing Blvd., and travel 9.8 miles. Turn left onto US 61 S. and go 11 miles. Turn left at the McDonald's, and then turn right onto N. Service Drive. In 0.4 mile parking will be on the left.

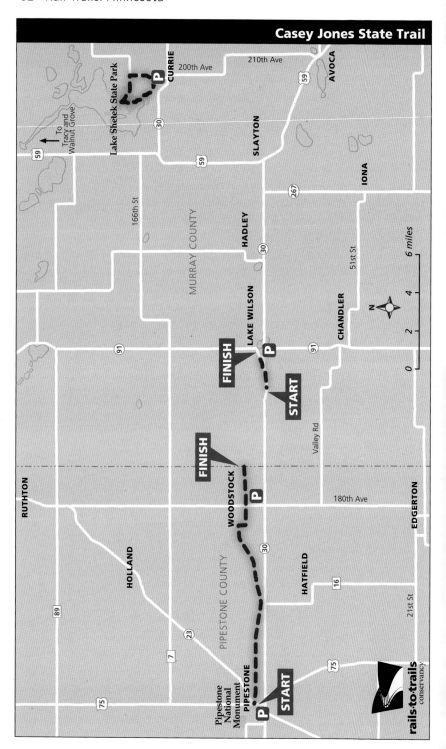

Three separate segments make up the Casey Jones State Trail, which is one of the first state trails authorized by Minnesota state trail legislation in the 1960s. The rail-trail is named for the engineer immortalized in the "Ballad of Casey Jones." In 1900 in Mississippi, the engineer "died at the throttle" when the train he was conducting collided with another train.

As for the trail itself, it courses through remnants of tallgrass prairie, providing glimpses of wind towers as it travels through woodland ravines amid a sea of agricultural land. The longest section, from Pipestone to just beyond Woodstock, occupies an inactive railroad corridor for 13 miles. This section is paved for 5 miles immediately east of Pipestone. The remaining 8 miles that continue to County Road 65 east of Woodstock are currently scheduled for grading and are being surfaced in aggregate.

Named for the engineer immortalized in "The Ballad of Casey Jones," trail segments connect users to Lake Shetek State Park and Lake Wilson.

Location
Murray, Pipestone

Endpoints
US 75 at MN 23 (Pipestone) to County Line Ave./County Road 65 at 111th St. (Woodstock); MN 30 at 40th Ave./CR 26 to corner of Ravine St. and Minnesota Ave. (Lake Wilson); Mill St., 0.3 mile south of 161st St., to Lake Shetek State Park at CR 96 and CR 37 (Currie)

Mileage 20.5

Type Rail-Trail

Roughness Index
1 (approximately 12.5 miles); 3 (approximately 8 miles)

Surface
Asphalt, Grass, Gravel

Another section runs from CR 26 east for just 1.5 miles into the small town of Lake Wilson.

The third section, which is entirely paved, forms a 6-mile loop from the tiny city of Currie to Lake Shetek State Park. This portion of the Casey Jones State Trail is wheelchair accessible; horses are not allowed. Trail users who want a bit of history may be interested in nearby attractions, including the Laura Ingalls Wilder museum in Walnut Grove; museums in Currie and Tracy that feature displays of railroad artifacts; and Pipestone National Monument, located about 1.5 miles from the Pipestone trailhead, which highlights the history of local American Indian quarries. In the future, the three disparate segments will be linked through a coordinated effort between the Minnesota Department of Natural Resources and the counties in which the segments are located, although there are no formal plans for construction at this time.

CONTACT: dnr.state.mn.us/state_trails/casey_jones

DIRECTIONS

To reach the trailhead in Pipestone, from I-90, take Exit 1 in Minnesota. Follow MN 23 north 28.5 miles. Turn right onto 101st St., and in 0.2 mile turn left onto Eighth Ave. N.E. In 0.6 mile turn right just before the intersection with MN 23, and take the immediate next left on a side road to access parking for the trail.

In Woodstock, access the trail at the community park on East St. From I-90, take Exit 1 in Minnesota. Follow MN 23 north 28.5 miles. Turn right onto 101st St./MN 30, and go 10.4 miles. Turn left onto 180th Ave., and in 1.2 miles turn right onto Third Ave. In 0.2 mile turn left onto East St., and the park will be on your right. Alternatively, from I-90, take Exit 26. Follow MN 91 north 24.6 miles. Turn left onto MN 30/Center Ave., and in 7.9 miles, turn right onto 180th Ave. Follow the directions above beginning on 180th.

Access the trail in Lake Wilson at the community park on First St. E. From I-90, take Exit 26. Follow MN 91 north 24.6 miles. Turn left onto Center Ave., and in 0.3 mile turn right onto Broadway Ave. In 0.3 mile turn right onto First St. E., and the park will be on your right.

To access the paved loop, park in Currie at End-O-Line Railroad Park and Museum off Mill St., just south of the trailhead. From I-90, take Exit 43. Follow US 59/N. Humiston Ave. 22.6 miles north. Turn right onto N.E. Second St., and take the first left onto Grand Ave., which becomes 210th Ave., then 121st St., and then 200th Ave. Follow it 9 miles, and turn left onto MN 30. In 0.1 mile turn right onto Mill St. In 0.6 mile the park will be on your right, and the trail is on your left.

You can also park at Lake Shetek State Park. To reach the state park, follow the directions above to Mill St. Follow Mill St. 2 miles, as it becomes 200th Ave. Turn left onto County Road 37/State Park Road, and go 1.7 miles to the state park.

The Cedar Lake Light Rail Transit (LRT) Regional Trail is an integral component of Hennepin County's extensive trail network, in which rail-trails feature prominently. The trail directly links four trails together: In the west, it branches off at the junction of both the similarly named North Cedar Lake Regional Trail and the Minnesota River Bluffs LRT Regional Trail. The eastern end of the Cedar Lake LRT Regional Trail seamlessly becomes Minneapolis's popular Midtown Greenway just north of Excelsior Boulevard, where Chowen Avenue South curves to become Abbott Avenue South. Just a few hundred yards north, it links up with the Kenilworth Trail (whose southern segment is also known as the Burnham Trail). Taking the Kenilworth Trail north enables users to link up with the North Cedar Lake Regional Trail and continue into downtown Minneapolis for even more trail connections. Heading back west along the North Cedar

Plans are in the works for the trail to share its entire length with a light rail line.

Location
Hennepin

Endpoints
Excelsior Blvd. and Jackson Ave. N. (Hopkins) to Kenilworth Trail and Midtown Greenway north of W. Lake St. (Minneapolis)

Mileage
4.5

Type
Rail-Trail

Roughness Index
1

Surface
Asphalt

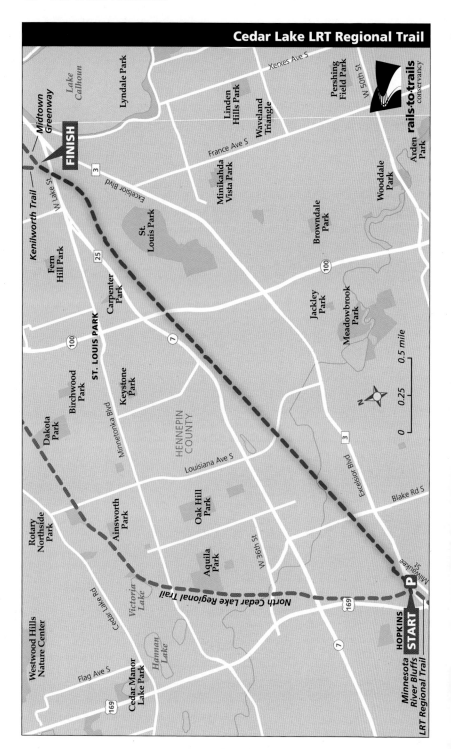

Cedar Lake LRT Regional Trail

rails-to-trails conservancy

Lake Calhoun

Lyndale Park

Xerxes Ave S

Pershing Field Park

W 50th St

Midtown Greenway

FINISH

Linden Hills Park

Waveland Triangle

France Ave S

Arden Park

Kenilworth Trail

3

W Lake St

Minikahda Vista Park

Wooddale Park

Excelsior Blvd

Fern Hill Park

St. Louis Park

Brerndale Park

Browndale Park

25

100

Carpenter Park

7

Jackley Park

Meadowbrook Park

ST. LOUIS PARK

100

Birchwood Park

Keystone Park

Minnetonka Blvd

HENNEPIN COUNTY

N

0   0.25   0.5 mile

Dakota Park

Louisiana Ave S

3

Rotary Northside Park

Ainsworth Park

Oak Hill Park

Excelsior Blvd

Blake Rd S

Westwood Hills Nature Center

Cedar Lake Rd S

Victoria Lake

Aquila Park

W 36th St

North Cedar Lake Regional Trail

Milwaukee St

P

HOPKINS

START

169

Cedar Manor Lake Park

Hannan Lake

Flag Ave S

7

169

Minnesota River Bluffs LRT Regional Trail

Lake Regional Trail leads to the western terminus in Hopkins as part of the 12-mile Cedar Lake Loop.

Running past mostly industrial properties, the 12-foot-wide, paved Cedar Lake LRT Regional Trail occupies a former Minneapolis and St. Louis Railway (and later Chicago and North Western Railway) corridor. The right-of-way became inactive in the early 1990s and was acquired by the Hennepin County Regional Railroad Authority (HCRRA), which installed the trail. The HCRRA always planned to use the corridor for a future passenger rail line; in fact, the LRT designation of several Hennepin County trails indicates those pathways built on corridors intended for future light rail transit use.

Fortunately, even though the planned Southwest LRT line will run on the entirety of what is now the Cedar Lake LRT Regional Trail, the HCRRA has committed to maintaining all existing trails. In this case, the trail will become one of an ever-increasing number of successful rail-with-trail projects around the country.

CONTACT: threeriversparks.org/trails/cedar-lake-trail.aspx

DIRECTIONS

To begin at the western end of the Cedar Lake LRT Regional Trail in Hopkins, park at the Depot Coffee House and trailhead, which lies immediately south of the trail on a spur that connects to the Minnesota River Bluffs LRT Regional Trail between Excelsior Blvd. and Milwaukee St. Take I-394 to Exit 3, and follow US 169 4.2 miles south. Take the Excelsior Blvd./County Road 3 exit. Turn left onto Excelsior Blvd. The coffee house will be on your right in 0.2 mile. The trail begins across the road.

Heading east out of Hopkins, there is also a large parking lot at the Sam's Club, immediately north of the trail access, on Louisiana Ave. S. in St. Louis Park. Take I-394 to Exit 5, and merge onto MN 100. Follow it 1.8 miles south, and take the W. 36th St. exit. Turn right onto Wooddale Ave. S., and in 0.4 mile turn left onto MN 7. In 0.3 mile take the Louisiana Ave. exit. Turn left onto Louisiana Ave., and in 0.1 mile Sam's Club will be on the left. The trail is at the southern end of the parking lot.

For access to the eastern end, take I-394 to Exit 5, and merge onto MN 100. Follow it 1.4 miles south, and take the CR 5/Minnetonka Blvd. exit. Turn left onto Minnetonka Blvd., and go 0.9 mile. Turn left onto CR 25, and in 0.6 mile make a sharp right onto Excelsior Blvd. Turn right onto Abbott Ave., where you can likely find parking along the street. The trail is in 0.2 mile, where Abbott meets Chowen Ave.

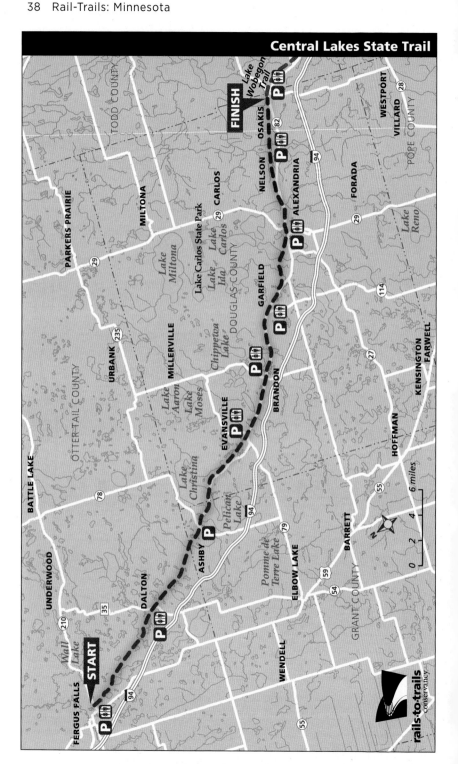

Central Lakes State Trail

The completion of the final segment of the Central Lakes State Trail in 2005 was the culmination of a positive partnership between volunteers and local and state officials that began in 1992 with the purchase, by the State of Minnesota, of an inactive Burlington Northern Railroad corridor.

The trail begins in Fergus Falls in Otter Tail County and ends in Osakis in Douglas County 55 miles to the south. The official northern trailhead has been an undeveloped parking lot just beyond where the trail crosses under MN 210. The Minnesota Department of Natural Resources has purchased property immediately south of MN 210 and, in the next few years, will be developing it as the official trailhead. For practical purposes of parking and limited water supply, trail users can park in Delagoon Park and take a short paved trail spur beyond the picnic area/campground to access the trail at that point (water is

The route passes through an incredibly diverse landscape, including dense forest, rolling hills, and historic Minnesota lakes.

Location
Douglas, Grant, Otter Tail

Endpoints
First Ave. E. and Main St. at Lake Wobegon Trail (Osakis) to MN 210 just east of E. Douglas Ave. (Fergus Falls)

Mileage
55

Type
Rail-Trail

Roughness Index
1

Surface
Asphalt

available only from sinks in the restrooms at the ballpark). There is also parking at a small gravel lot farther south just before the trail crosses County Road 29 at Chautauqua Lake.

The landscape between the two cities is incredibly diverse, ranging from rolling hills and dense forest to farmland, prairie remnants, and Minnesota's famous lakes. Because the trail runs past lakes used by many species of waterfowl during migration, bird-watching aficionados will want to bring their binoculars.

While much of the trail offers the kind of rural serenity that lends itself to bird-watching and wildlife sightings, it also passes many railroad and state historic sites. The paved pathway also runs directly through the city of Alexandria, just northeast of a small town where the Kensington Runestone, an alleged Viking artifact, was discovered. The urban route passes several miles of both commercial and residential areas before reentering a pastoral landscape. There are significant road crossings along this route, so caution is advised.

The small towns of Ashby, Garfield, Nelson, Brandon, and Evansville all offer convenience stores or cafés where you can grab a bite to eat. The trail is a spacious 14 feet wide for its entire length. In Osakis, the Central Lakes State Trail connects directly to the Lake Wobegon Trail. That trail continues south for another 62 miles to the city of St. Joseph.

CONTACT: centrallakestrail.com

DIRECTIONS

To reach the trail in Osakis, take I-94 to Exit 114. Head 1.9 miles northeast on MN 27, and turn left onto First Ave. E. In 0.7 mile turn left onto W. Main St. Park at the Osakis Information Center on the corner of Central Ave. and W. Main St.

To reach the trail in Fergus Falls at Delagoon Park, from I-94, take Exit 57. Head 1.7 miles north on MN 210 E. Turn right onto Pebble Lake Road, and go 0.9 mile. Turn left onto Delagoon Park Drive. Parking is on the left in 0.5 mile.

In the smaller cities of Dalton, Ashby, Evansville, Brandon, Garfield, Alexandria, and Nelson, park at the dedicated parking lots where available or on city streets.

The Cuyuna Lakes State Trail winds its way through northern hardwoods and spruce/pine forests along the shores of 6 natural lakes and 15 clear, constructed lakes that were former mine pits. The cluster of lakes has a combined undeveloped shoreline length of more than 25 miles.

The trail traverses the 5,000-acre Cuyuna Country State Recreation Area, featuring the world-class Cuyuna Mountain Bike Trail System with more than 25 miles of riding and 30 miles of purpose-built routes suited for beginner to professional riders.

When completed, the trail will encompass about 30 miles from Aitkin to Baxter, where it will connect to the Paul Bunyan State Trail. Currently, only the middle segment is open, from Riverton to Crosby. There is also a paved 1-mile segment in the city of Aitkin, 15 miles east of Crosby, that parallels US 169 through the center of the city and links into a loop of trails at Aitkin City Park at the trail's north end.

Most of the facilities along the trail are privately owned and operated. The Cuyuna Country State Recreation Area manages two Minnesota Department of Natural Resources forestry campgrounds nearby.

This gorgeous trail goes through many natural forests and passes by several crystal-clear lakes.

Location
Crow Wing

Endpoints
County Road 31/Cuyuna Road and Heartwood Drive (Crosby) to CR 128 and Main St. (Riverton)

Mileage
7

Type
Rail-Trail

Roughness Index
1

Surface
Asphalt

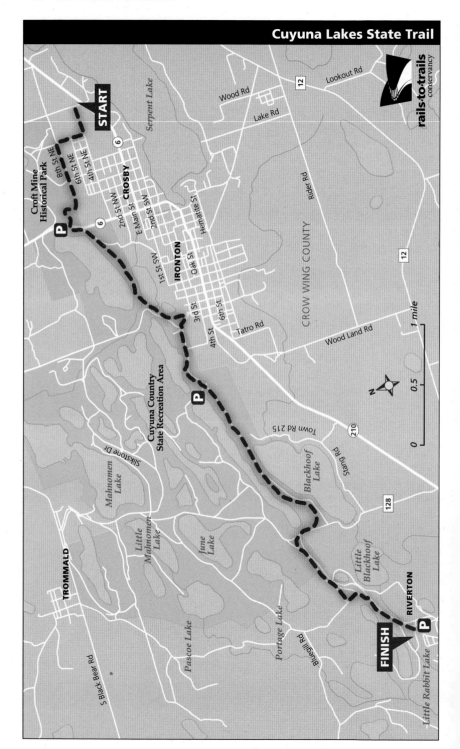

Cuyuna Lakes State Trail

Restrooms are available at the Portsmouth Campground, about 0.5 mile north of the trail on the east side of CR 30.

CONTACT: cuyunalakestrail.org

DIRECTIONS

From Minneapolis, take US 169 about 17 miles north, and turn left onto US 10/US 169. In 10.2 miles, exit right onto US 169. Travel 75.6 miles north on US 169 to Garrison. Turn left onto MN 18, and go 4.3 miles. Turn right onto MN 6, and go 9.5 miles. Turn left onto E. Front St., and in 0.4 mile turn right onto MN 6/MN 210/Archibald Road. In 2.9 miles turn right onto Cuyuna Road. In 0.3 mile turn left onto Eighth St. N.E. to reach Croft Mine Historical Park in 0.6 mile. Or go 0.4 mile on Eighth St. N.E. to park at the Hallett Center of Crosby, located at 470 Eighth St. N.E.

Just west of Crosby, parking is available in Cuyuna Country State Recreation Area off Portsmouth Mine Road. From Minneapolis, take US 169 about 17 miles north, and turn left onto US 10/US 169. In 10.2 miles, exit right onto US 169. Travel 75.6 miles north on US 169 to Garrison. Turn left onto MN 18, and go 4.3 miles. Turn right onto MN 6, and go 9.5 miles. Turn left onto Front St., and in 2.5 miles turn right onto County Road 28. In 1.5 miles turn left onto Oak St./MN 210. In 0.9 mile turn right onto Irene Ave. In 0.3 mile make a slight left, and continue 0.6 mile on Portsmouth Mine Road to parking on the right.

For the Riverton trailhead, from Minneapolis, take US 169 about 17 miles north, and turn left onto US 10/US 169. In 10.2 miles, exit right onto US 169. Travel 75.6 miles north on US 169 to Garrison. Turn left onto MN 18, and go 4.3 miles. Turn right onto MN 6, and go 9.5 miles. Turn left onto Front St., and go 7.2 miles. Turn left onto MN 210, and in 0.9 mile turn right onto County Road 59. Go 1 mile north on CR 59, and take a right onto CR 128. Take the first left onto Rowe Road, and the entrance to the parking lot is about 100 feet on the right.

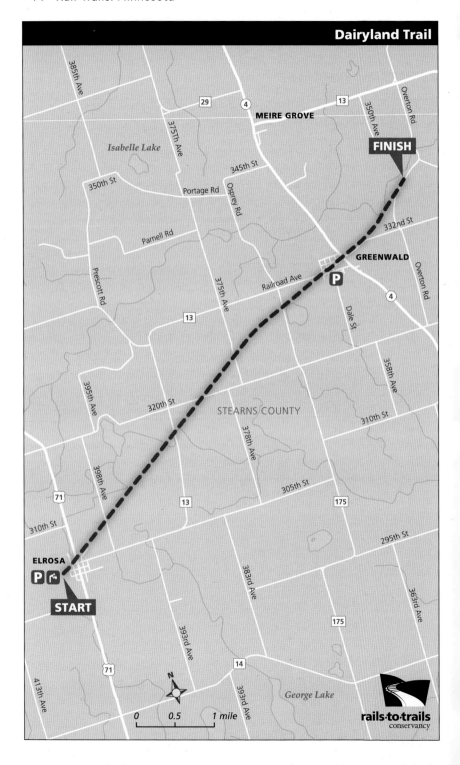

Dairyland Trail

Phase one of the development of central Minnesota's Dairyland Trail was completed in April 2013, allowing trail users to hike, bike, or ride a horse for more than 6 miles between the small towns of Elrosa and Greenwald. The trail, named in recognition of Stearns County's status as the top dairy producer in Minnesota, occupies a Soo Line Railroad corridor developed as a railroad in the early 1900s and rendered inactive in 1996. The trail will eventually stretch for 26 miles between Albany and Brooten.

The open portion of the trail passes through a landscape of cornfields, prairie remnants, and dairy farms. Small game and upland bird hunting is allowed on the trail, with specific restrictions determined by local ordinances.

When completed, the trail will link directly with the paved Lake Wobegon Trail in Albany, which offers several other connections to trails throughout the heart of

This 6-mile trail connects the small towns of Elrosa and Greenwald in Stearns County.

Location
Stearns

Endpoints
Second Ave. and Stearns St. at the baseball field (Elrosa) to Overton Road, 0.3 mile west of 343rd Ave. (Melrose, 1 mile east of Greenwald)

Mileage
6.2

Type
Rail-Trail

Roughness Index
2

Surface
Crushed Stone

Minnesota. It will also become part of a regional snowmobile trail network; all-terrain vehicles will not be allowed on this trail.

Currently, all services and facilities (that is, parking, restaurants, restrooms, drinking water, and equestrian areas) are available only in the trailhead communities of Elrosa and Greenwald. Drinking water at the baseball field in Elrosa is available only during summer.

CONTACT: co.stearns.mn.us/recreation/trailsandconditions/dairylandtrailsooline

DIRECTIONS

Parking is available year-round in Elrosa (the current southern terminus of the trail) at the parking lot for the baseball field and trail on Second Ave. From I-94, take Exit 135. Head south on Second Ave. E./County Road 13, and drive 4.9 miles. Turn left onto MN 4, and in 2 miles, turn right onto W. Railroad Ave./CR 13. In 6.7 miles turn left onto Main St. Take the first right onto Second Ave., which dead-ends in 0.2 mile at the baseball field.

To reach the trail parking lot across from the Greenwald Pub in Greenwald, from I-94, take Exit 135. Head south on Second Ave. E./CR 13, and drive 4.9 miles. Turn left onto MN 4, and in 2 miles, turn right onto W. Railroad Ave. In 0.1 mile the parking lot will be on your left at S. Third St.

Sections of the Dakota Rail Regional Trail, which extends westward from the Minneapolis suburbs situated along Lake Minnetonka, have been opening since June 2009. The trail occupies the former Dakota Rail corridor, which ran for a total length of 44 miles to Hutchinson, Minnesota, before falling out of use in 2001. That same year, the Hennepin County Regional Railroad Authority, Carver County, and McLeod County jointly purchased the corridor with the goal of establishing a rail-trail. The 13-mile Hennepin County section of the trail begins at the lakefront in downtown Wayzata, an idyllic suburb of Minneapolis.

Lake views are never far away for much of the trail's journey through Hennepin County. In fact, many of these communities were developed in the late 19th century as popular resort towns because of their stunning views of the clear water and convenient location along the expanding

Enjoy the serene beauty along the path in Carver County.

Location
Carver, Hennepin

Endpoints
Grove Lane E. just east of Ferndale Road S. (Wayzata) to MN 9 and MN 185/County Road 23 (Lester Prairie)

Mileage
25.5

Type
Rail-Trail

Roughness Index
1

Surface
Asphalt

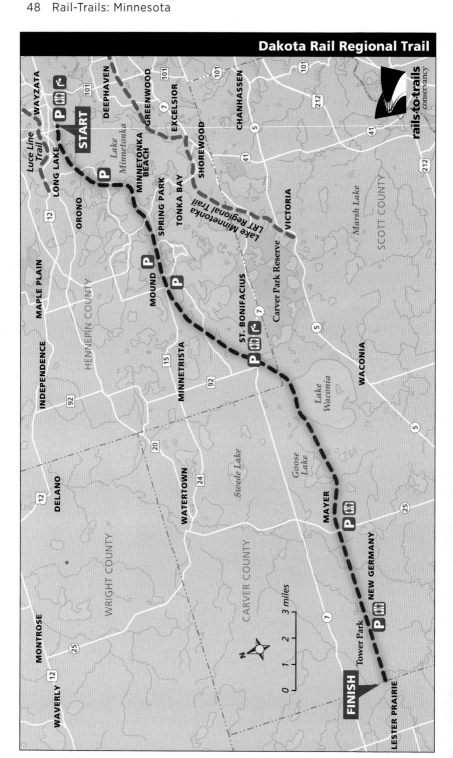

Dakota Rail Regional Trail

rails-to-trails
conservancy

railroad lines. These towns, which are now largely residential, include Orono, Minnetonka Beach, Spring Park, and Mound. After passing through the town of St. Bonifacius, the trail enters Carver County.

The section of trail from the border with Hennepin County in the east to the small city of Mayer in the west was constructed in 2010. Like the first portion of the trail, striking lake views, now of vast Lake Waconia, make up much of the scenery. After the lake, the trail passes through an equally beautiful mix of open fields and forest.

The newest section of the Dakota Rail Regional Trail opened in early 2013. Running from Mayer to the Carver–McLeod county line, the trail parallels a lightly used rural road. Trail users pass through the tiny town of New Germany before reaching the current western endpoint. Work to upgrade and gravel the section of the trail extending from the McLeod–Carver county line into the town of Lester Prairie was in progress in the fall of 2015. Funding is being sought to pave this section. Development plans extend the paved trail all the way to Hutchinson, the largest city in McLeod County. Currently, the trail west of Lester Prairie is used primarily as an all-terrain vehicle/snowmobile trail.

CONTACT: threeriversparks.org/trails/dakota-rail-trail.aspx and
co.carver.mn.us/departments/public-works/parks-recreation
/parks-trails/regional-trails

DIRECTIONS

To begin in Wayzata, from the intersection of I-494 and I-394, follow US 12 W. 1.6 miles, and take the exit for County Road 101 S. (toward Wayzata). Continue onto Bushaway Road/Gleason Lake Drive, and take the first right onto Wayzata Blvd. E. In 1.1 miles turn left onto Barry Ave. and in 0.2 mile continue onto Grove Lane E. In 0.2 mile designated trail parking spaces will be on your left in Shaver Park (175 Grove Lane).

In Mound, park at the downtown transit center adjoining the trail at the intersection of Lynwood Blvd. and Commerce Blvd. From the intersection of I-494 and I-394, follow US 12 W. 3.3 miles, and take the CR 15 W. exit. Merge onto CR 15/Shoreline Drive, and go 7.7 miles. The transit center will be on your left.

Parking is available in St. Bonifacius at Don Logelin Memorial Lions Park, located on Bell St. just off MN 7. From I-494, take Exit 16B. Follow MN 7 W. 15.8 miles. Turn right onto Bell St., and the trail is on the right.

Parking is also available in downtown New Germany on Broadway St. From I-494, take Exit 16B. Follow MN 7 W. 22 miles. Turn left onto MN 25, and in 1.8 miles turn right onto CR 30/ First St. N.E. In 3.7 miles parking will be on the left.

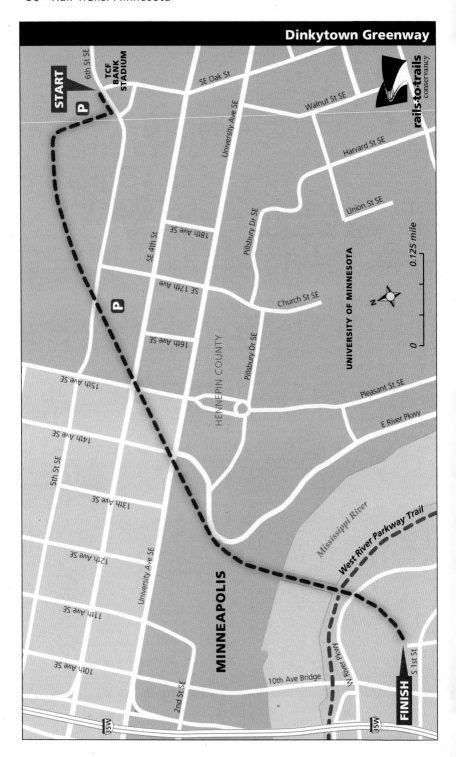

Dinkytown Greenway

Although only 1 mile long, the Dinkytown Greenway provides an important link in a biking network connecting Minneapolis and Saint Paul. The trail begins near TCF Bank Stadium and runs through the University of Minnesota campus on the east bank of the Mississippi River. On the east side of the stadium, a connection can be made to the University of Minnesota transit, which connects the school's Minneapolis and Saint Paul campuses.

Part of the Dinkytown Greenway runs through a former railroad trench with the Dinkytown community (after which the trail is named) visible overhead. A pedestrian staircase has been proposed that will connect the greenway trench segment with Dinkytown proper. As the trail heads west, it crosses Bridge No. 9, once used by the Northern Pacific Railway but now open for bicyclists and pedestrians.

The bridge yields quite spectacular views. The view upriver includes a glimpse of St. Anthony Falls and the

Location
Hennepin

Endpoints
S.E. Oak St. and Fifth
St. S.E. to 20th Ave. S.
(Minneapolis)

Mileage
1

Type
Rail-Trail

Roughness Index
1

Surface
Asphalt

View of Minneapolis's downtown skyline from Bridge No. 9

famed Stone Arch Bridge, while the view to the east overlooks the Bohemian Flats segment of the West River Parkway Trail.

The trail ends on the river's west bank, where it merges with the West River Parkway Trail and lies within short access to the St. Anthony Falls Heritage Trail. The addition of the Bluff Street bicycle tunnel under I-35W to 13th Avenue South provides a smooth transition to the West River Parkway Trail, the historic Mill District, and other sections of downtown Minneapolis.

If you leave the greenway/parkway along the river, you can cross over the 10th Avenue Bridge and head back over the river to access University Avenue just west of Dinkytown and the University of Minnesota campus.

CONTACT: dinkytowngreenway.org

DIRECTIONS

Access to the east trailhead is north of University Ave. at Oak St., with ample parking in the University of Minnesota Maroon Lot (2028 Sixth St. S.E.) or Lot 37 (1811 Fifth St. S.E.). Take I-35W N. to Exit 18. Head 0.4 mile southeast on University Ave. S.E. Turn left onto 15th Ave. S.E., and in 0.1 mile turn right onto Fifth St. S.E. Lot 37 is in 0.3 mile on the left, and the Maroon Lot is 0.5 mile on the right.

Parking south of Bridge No. 9 is randomly available along 20th Ave. S., S. First St., and other neighborhood streets in the vicinity. Get to this area by taking I-35W N. to Exit 18. Head southeast on University Ave., and immediately turn right onto 10th Ave. Bridge. In 0.4 mile turn left onto S. 19th Ave. or right onto S. Second St. A parking lot is also on the east side of the West Bank Fields ball diamond at S. First St. and 21st Ave. S.

The Douglas State Trail occupies the railbed of the former Chicago Great Western Railway corridor between the cities of Rochester and Pine Island. Several of the concrete obelisk railroad mile markers are still visible along parts of the route.

Along the trail, users are treated to a diverse, bucolic landscape of verdant agricultural land, rolling fields, and forest. Not far from Rochester, the trail passes through its namesake town of Douglas. The trail is paved over its entire route, but there is also a parallel natural-surface treadway for horseback riders and snowmobilers. In Rochester, connect directly with the Douglas-Cascade Trail to continue farther into Rochester's extensive 60-mile trail system within the city.

The trail crosses over the Zumbro River and two creeks along the route as it winds through a canopy of hardwoods

A canopy of hardwood trees shades the path.

Location
Goodhue, Olmsted

Endpoints
Center Drive between First Ave. N.E. and Third Ave. N.E. (Pine Island) to Valleyhigh Drive N.W. near Prow Lane N.W. at Douglas-Cascade Trail (Rochester)

Mileage
12.5

Type
Rail-Trail

Roughness Index
1

Surface
Asphalt

Douglas State Trail

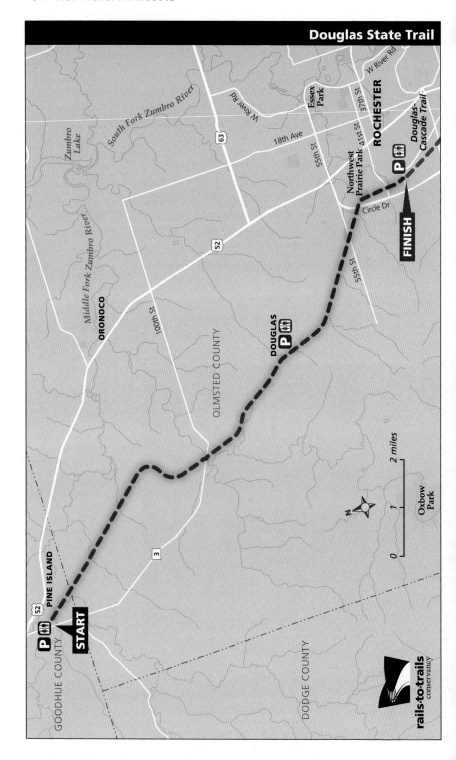

lining the trail. It also passes by, and through, working farms, mixing agriculture with nature along its route. Recently widened and repaved, the trail provides a smooth, flat ride throughout. Two bridges damaged in the floods of 2010 closed the trail for two years but have since been repaired.

Just before crossing County Road 3, about 4 miles south of Pine Island, you can rest at a shelter next to the trail. There is a gravel parking lot providing access to the trail from New Haven Road. A couple of benches at other points on the trail provide convenient rest stops along the route.

Ample parking and services at each major trailhead make it easy to enjoy segments of this trail: about 8 miles between Douglas and Pine Island to the north or the 4-mile stretch between Rochester and Douglas in the southern segment.

Several county roads (some gravel) intersect this trail along its course, providing short-looped excursions off the main route. There is often limited parking at these intersections.

The Pine Island trailhead offers a Borrow-a-Bike program for those who would like to ride the trail.

CONTACT: dnr.state.mn.us/state_trails/douglas

DIRECTIONS

Three trailheads along the route provide parking and restrooms, and all are accessible within a few miles from US 52.

To reach the northern trailhead from Saint Paul, go 59.7 miles south on US 52, and take the County Road 11 exit. Turn right onto Center Drive, and in 0.5 mile turn left onto First Ave. N.E. Pine Island City Park is on the left.

To reach the Douglas trailhead midway along the trail, from Saint Paul, go 69.1 miles south on US 52, and take Exit 61 for US 63/CR 14/75th St. N.W. Turn right onto 75th St. N.W./CR 14, and go 2.6 miles. Parking is on the left.

To reach the southern trailhead in Rochester, from Saint Paul, go 71.2 miles south on US 52, and take Exit 59 for CR 22 W./W. Circle Drive/55th St. N.W. Turn right onto 55th St. N.W./W. Circle Drive, and go 2 miles. Turn left onto Valleyhigh Drive N.W. in Rochester. The parking lot will be on your left in 0.2 mile.

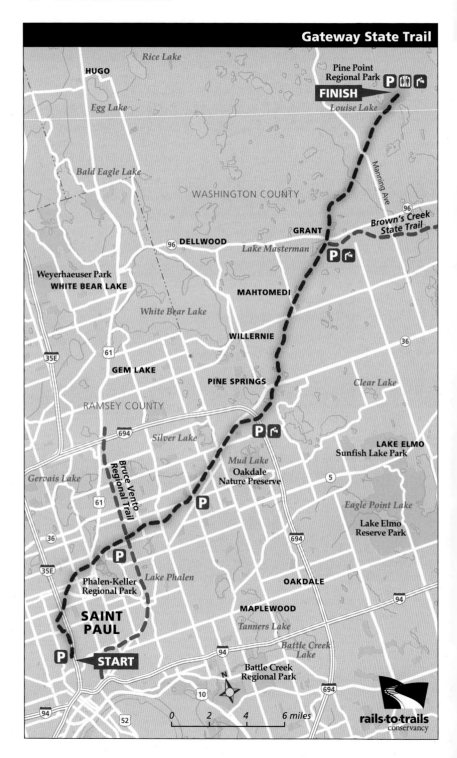

Gateway State Trail

The Gateway State Trail is an 18.3-mile-long path-way that offers an urban link to the countryside. The western end of this paved trail begins on the north end of Saint Paul and heads northeast through urban and suburban landscapes along 8 miles of tree-lined corri-dors to the eastern edges of residential communities. As you approach Pine Springs, the mid-trail access point on 55th Street, just east of Hadley Avenue, offers ample parking and a good starting point for the more scenic and bucolic section of the Gateway State Trail's eastern segment. Once it crosses under I-694 at the junction with MN 36, the trail continues eastward for another 10 miles through the countryside to Pine Point Regional Park. The trail offers a superb mix of parks, lakes, wet-lands, and Midwestern northern prairie lands.

Multiple winter uses, including snowmobiling, are per-mitted along the Gateway State Trail. A 10-mile section of

Cyclists frequent the bicycle tune-up stations along the trail.

Location
Ramsey, Washington

Endpoints
Cayuga Park at L'Orient St. and E. Cayuga St. (Saint Paul) to Pine Point Regional Park at Norell Ave. N. south of 120th St. N. (Stillwater)

Mileage
18.3

Type
Rail-Trail

Roughness Index
1

Surface
Asphalt (adjacent horse-back trail is Crushed Stone)

parallel gravel trail is also available for horseback riding along a segment located between I-694 and Pine Point Regional Park. The paved section of trail through here is groomed during the winter for cross-country skiers. Permits are required for horseback riding, carriage driving, and cross-country skiing.

The Gateway State Trail, built on the former right-of-way of the Soo Line Railroad, connects to trails in Phalen-Keller Regional Park, the Bruce Vento Regional Trail in Saint Paul, and Brown's Creek State Trail, which links the Gateway State Trail east to Stillwater along the old Zephyr line.

The trail enters Pine Point Regional Park at its western boundary and links up with a network of trails within the park. An extension of the trail from the Stillwater area to William O'Brien State Park approximately 6 miles to the north is proposed for future development.

As of spring 2016, construction/repairs have closed the Gateway State Trail near the western trailhead in the section between L'Orient and Cayuga Streets. The trail has been temporarily rerouted along L'Orient Street, Maryland Avenue, Jackson Street, and Cayuga Street. The Gateway State Trail should reopen in the Cayuga area sometime in the summer of 2016. As part of the I-35E/Cayuga project, the trail is being extended from Cayuga Street to University Avenue.

A Minnesota Department of Natural Resources bicycle tune-up station has been installed at the intersection of the Gateway State Trail and the Bruce Vento Regional Trail. Another station, purchased by the Gateway–Brown's Creek Trail Association, has been installed at the Hadley Avenue access point.

Restrooms are located at the 55th Street/Hadley Avenue access, MN 96 under the trail bridge, Lansing Avenue (May–October only), Pine Point Regional Park, and other adjacent city and regional parks along the route.

CONTACT: gatewaybrownscreektrail.org

DIRECTIONS

To reach the southern parking lot at Cayuga Park in Saint Paul (198 Cayuga St.): From I-35E, take Exit 109 onto Maryland Ave. E. Head east for 0.5 mile and turn left onto Jackson St.; travel 0.7 mile south and turn left onto Cayuga St. You will see the entrance to the parking lot in Cayuga Park on your right after 0.2 mile. From the parking lot, continue in the same direction of travel (east) along the sidewalk until you reach L'Orient St. a short distance away; you'll see a sign indicating the beginning of the trail on your left.

To reach the northern parking lot at Pine Point Regional Park (11900 Norell Ave. N., Stillwater): From I-694 take Exit 52B. Merge onto MN 36 E., and go 5.1 miles east. Turn left onto Manning Ave. N., and in 3 miles, turn right onto MN 96/Dellwood Road. In 1.6 miles turn left onto County Road 55/Norell Ave. N., and drive 3 miles. Turn left into the park. Note that a daily permit of $5 is required for motorized vehicles entering the park.

When completed, the Gitchi-Gami State Trail will traverse 88 paved miles between the cities of Two Harbors and Grand Marais on Lake Superior's northern shore. Currently, several segments, totaling nearly 29 miles, are open between the two endpoints. A "West Road" section, forecast for completion in 2016, will extend the trail northward along the shore of Lake Superior, completing the connection to the community of Silver Bay. The trail provides a nonmotorized, safer alternative to MN 61 along the North Shore.

The Gitchi-Gami Trail Association's mission is to promote, plan, and construct the trail to link communities, state parks, and points of interest along the northern shore of Lake Superior. Trail segments pass through five Minnesota state parks along the North Shore, winding through birch and aspen forests, along cascading rivers and waterfalls, and through historic communities, while providing incredible vistas of Gitchi-Gami herself, Lake Superior.

There are currently six segments completed along the planned 88-mile route: Silver Creek Cliff features more

Currently, the trail's completed segments pass through five state parks along the shore of Lake Superior.

Location
Cook, Lake

Endpoints
Silver Cliff Road and MN 61 (Two Harbors) to Outer Drive and Horn Blvd. (Silver Bay); MN 61 and County Road 32 (Schroeder) to MN 61 and Sugar Beach Drive (Tofte); MN 61 and Sawbill Trail to MN 61 and Ski Hill Road (Tofte); MN 61 and Fall River Road/CR 13 to First Ave. W. and Wisconsin St. (Grand Marais)

Mileage
28.6

Type
Greenway/Non-Rail-Trail

Roughness Index
1

Surface
Asphalt

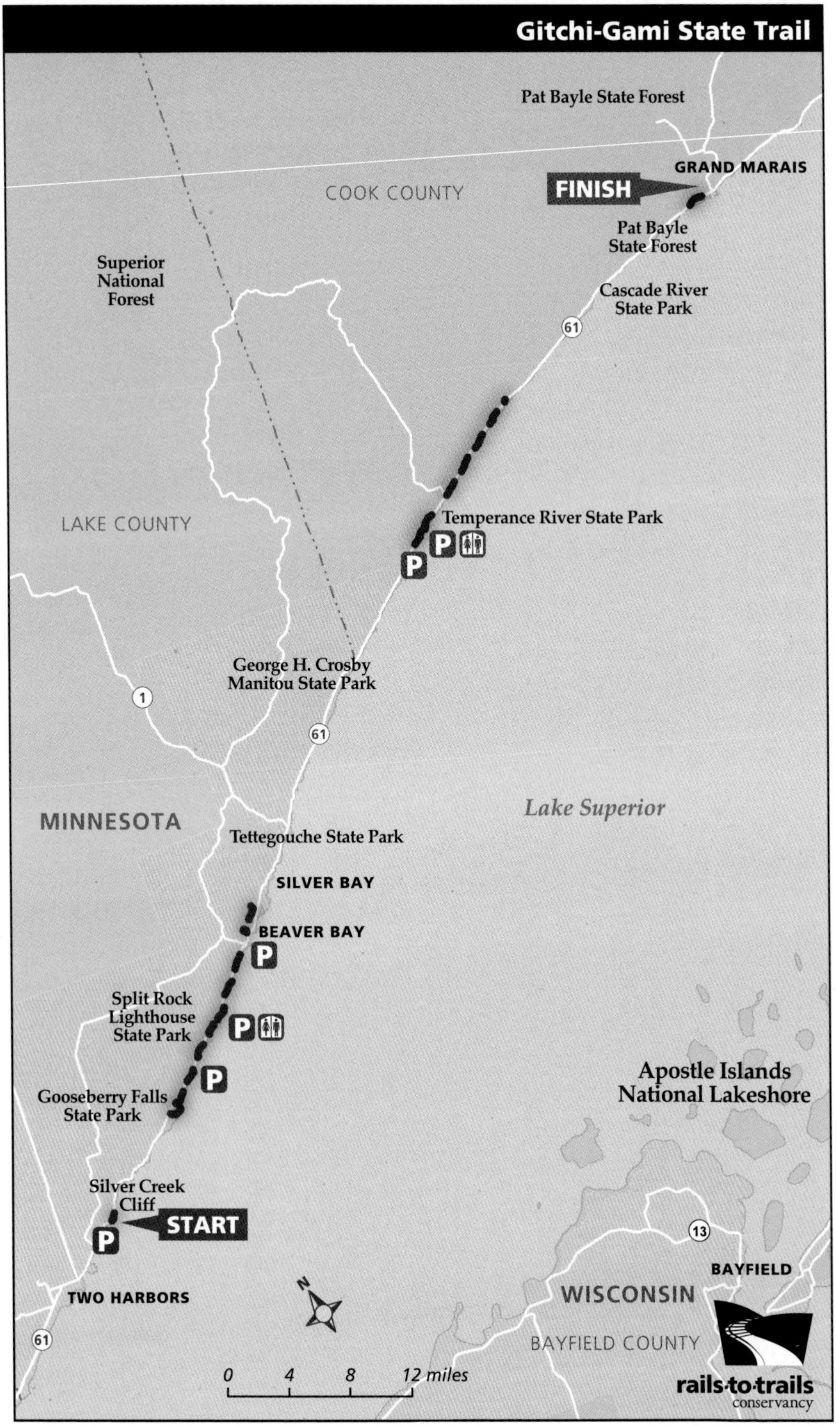

Gitchi-Gami State Trail

Pat Bayle State Forest

COOK COUNTY

FINISH GRAND MARAIS

Pat Bayle
State Forest

Superior
National
Forest

Cascade River
State Park

61

LAKE COUNTY

George H. Crosby
Manitou State Park

Temperance River State Park

P P 🚻

P

1

61

MINNESOTA

Lake Superior

Tettegouche State Park

SILVER BAY

BEAVER BAY

P

Split Rock
Lighthouse
State Park

P 🚻

P

Gooseberry Falls
State Park

Silver Creek
Cliff

START

Apostle Islands
National Lakeshore

13

P

BAYFIELD

TWO HARBORS

N

WISCONSIN

61

BAYFIELD COUNTY

0   4   8   12 miles

rails·to·trails
conservancy

than 4,000 feet of continuous vista along its short 1-mile section just north of Two Harbors, along MN 61. The longest section begins at Gooseberry Falls State Park and runs 14.6 miles to Beaver Bay, with a sometimes steep and curving trail that is considered the most scenic portion of the completed trail segments.

A 2.3-mile section from the community of East Beaver Bay north to Silver Bay cuts inland, paralleling the Northshore Mining Railroad. From the ridgeline above Lake Superior, the route offers spectacular views of the region. The Temperance River segment connects the 3 miles between the towns of Schroeder and Tofte. At Tofte, the trail continues northward along the shore for another 7.4 miles, ending at County Road 5 (also known as Ski Hill Road).

The last completed segment of the trail runs west 1.5 miles from the western edge of Grand Marais. It connects with the Grand Marais Corridor Trail at Eighth Avenue to provide another 0.5 mile to the northern end of the Gitchi-Gami State Trail network along the shore.

Bicycle tune-up stations have been installed at Gooseberry Falls State Park behind the visitor center along the trail and at Split Rock Lighthouse State Park near the park office.

Restrooms are available at each of the state parks along the trail and in each town or community along the route.

CONTACT: ggta.org

DIRECTIONS

Parking is available in Two Harbors on the east side of the Silver Creek Cliff Tunnel off MN 61. Take I-35 to Exit 259. Merge onto MN 61 N./London Road, and go 29.4 miles northeast. Just after you go through the tunnel, the parking will be on your right.

Additional parking can be found in Gooseberry Falls State Park at the Picnic Flow parking lot (37.3 miles along MN 61 from the interstate), at Twin Points Protected Access in Silver Creek (40.3 miles along MN 61 from the interstate), and the trail center off MN 61 in Split Rock Lighthouse State Park (43.4 miles along MN 61 from the interstate). Parking is also available at the trailhead parking lot in Beaver Bay, 51.1 miles along MN 61 from the interstate.

In Silver Bay, parking can be found adjacent to Rukavina (hockey) Arena on Outer Drive. Take I-35 to Exit 259. Merge onto MN 61 N./London Road, and go 52.4 miles northeast. Turn left onto Outer Drive, and the parking lot will be on your right in 1 mile.

To reach the trailhead in Schroeder, take I-35 to Exit 259. Merge onto MN 61 N./London Road, and go 78.9 miles northeast. The parking lot will be on the left. Parking is available 1 mile farther at Temperance River State Park.

To reach the trailhead in Grand Marais, take I-35 to Exit 259. Merge onto MN 61 N./London Road, and go 107 miles northeast. Turn right onto Wisconsin St. and park along city streets.

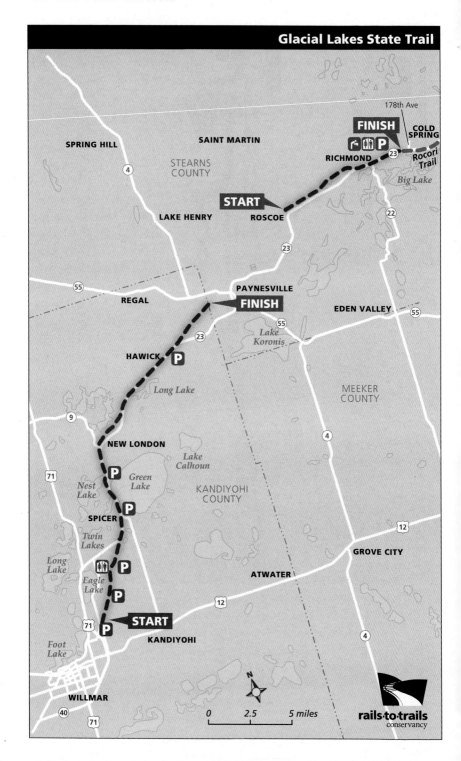

Glacial Lakes State Trail

The 22-mile original section of the paved Glacial Lakes State Trail follows the former right-of-way of the Burlington Northern Railroad between Willmar and about 1 mile west of Paynesville at Roseville Road Northeast, at the Kandiyohi–Stearns county line. The trail passes through the towns of Spicer, New London, and Hawick and past Green Lake. The segment between Willmar and Spicer includes a 10-mile parallel grass track for equestrians, and the rest of the trail includes a grassy shoulder for equestrians.

The trail traverses the gently rolling prairies of central Minnesota and travels between a landscape of tallgrass prairie and deciduous forest. Among the farmlands, you can catch glimpses of the original prairie and wetlands, which make ideal habitat for white-tailed deer, small mammals, birds, reptiles, and butterflies.

The Minnesota Department of Natural Resources (DNR) recently installed a bike repair station unit at the Civic Center trailhead in Willmar. The City of Willmar has also developed this area to include an information kiosk and a rack with bikes for free use throughout the city.

Deciduous forest and wetlands compose the landscape of this 22-mile paved trail.

Location
Kandiyohi, Stearns

Endpoints
Civic Center Drive and County Road 9 (Willmar) to Roseville Road N.E. and 262nd Ave. N.E. (Paynesville); Main St. and First St. (Roscoe) to 178th Ave. and MN 23 (Cold Spring)

Mileage
30

Type
Rail-Trail

Roughness Index
1, 3

Surface
Asphalt

In New London, you can take a side trip to Sibley State Park (about 3 miles away); follow MN 9 to County Road 148. Note: If you go by bike, you will have to ride in a bike lane on the shoulder of CR 148. In Paynesville you can connect to city trails that circle Lake Koronis. Services are available in the towns along the route, including rest areas and restrooms. The trail is groomed for snowmobiles during winter in Kandiyohi County.

Beyond the county line near Paynesville, the trail is undeveloped to Roscoe; railroad ballast still covers the surface, and some bridges are out. From Roscoe, a newer 5-mile paved segment takes trail users to Richmond, where water and restrooms are available at the new Glacial Lakes Pavilion.

Just east of Richmond, the Glacial Lakes State Trail continues to 178th Avenue, where it seamlessly connects to the Rocori Trail. The Rocori Trail will eventually continue to Rockville, and long-term planning extends the trail all the way into St. Cloud. Note that snowmobiling is prohibited on the Stearns County section of the Glacial Lakes State Trail.

CONTACT: dnr.state.mn.us/state_trails/glacial_lakes

DIRECTIONS

You can access Glacial Lakes State Trail in many places along its route.

In Willmar, take I-94 to Exit 127. Head south on MN 28 W./US 71 S./Main St. S., and go 20.3 miles. Turn left onto US 71, and go 20.6 miles. Turn left onto 37th Ave. N.E./County Road 90, and in 0.7 mile turn right onto 30th St. N.E./CR 9 N.E. Turn right onto Civic Center Drive; parking will be on your right.

For the parking in Spicer, take I-94 to Exit 127. Head south on MN 28 W./US 71 S./Main St. S., and go 20.3 miles. Turn left onto US 71, and go 15.3 miles. Turn left onto CR 10/113th Ave. N.E., and go 2.7 miles. Turn left onto Agnes St., and in 0.1 mile see the parking lot across Second Ave.

Another parking area in Spicer is located on the south side of the bridge over the channel between Nest and Green Lakes. Take I-94 to Exit 127. Head south on MN 28 W./US 71 S./Main St. S., and go 20.3 miles. Turn left onto US 71, and go 10.8 miles. Turn left onto CR 40/180th Ave. N.W., and go 3.1 miles. Turn right onto MN 9/Main St. In 0.4 mile turn right onto MN 23, and go 2 miles. Turn right onto CR 30, and take the first right to reach the parking lot.

Construction scheduled in the near future on MN 23 includes relocating the trail parking lot in Hawick to the south side of the highway. To reach it, take I-94 to Exit 147. Head south on Eighth St. S., and in 0.2 mile turn right onto CR 10. In 0.3 mile turn left to stay on CR 10, and go 14.9 miles. Merge onto MN 23, and in 12.4 miles, if construction has been completed, turn left onto 160th St. N.E. to reach the parking lot. If construction is not complete, turn right onto 160th Ave. N.E., and parking will be on the left.

No good parking is available from Roscoe to Richmond.

The Goodhue Pioneer State Trail is a work in progress as part of a planned 47-mile trail linking the cities of Red Wing, Goodhue, Zumbrota, Mazeppa, Bellechester, and Pine Island along an inactive railroad corridor. The Duluth, Red Wing & Southern Railroad constructed the line in the late 1880s. However, a derailment in 1964 caused the line to be embargoed by the Chicago Great Western Railroad.

Currently, two sections of trail, separated by a 12-mile gap, are open for recreational use. The 4.2-mile northern segment begins at Pioneer Road on the southern edge of Red Wing. The trail follows Hay Creek as it winds through the Richard J. Dorer Memorial Hardwood State Forest. Rugged hills blanketed in hardwood forests of oak, elm, birch, black cherry, and basswood dominate the landscape. An adjacent unpaved trail allows for equestrian use.

Minnesota's last remaining original covered bridge in Zumbrota

Location
Goodhue

Endpoints
Pioneer Road and Hay Creek Valley Road to Hay Creek Valley Campground at Hay Creek Trail and MN 58 (Red Wing); Covered Bridge Park on MN 58 (Zumbrota) to 180th Ave. at 410th St. (Minneola)

Mileage
9.7 (4.2-mile northern section; 5.5-mile southern section)

Type
Rail-Trail

Roughness Index
1

Surface
Asphalt

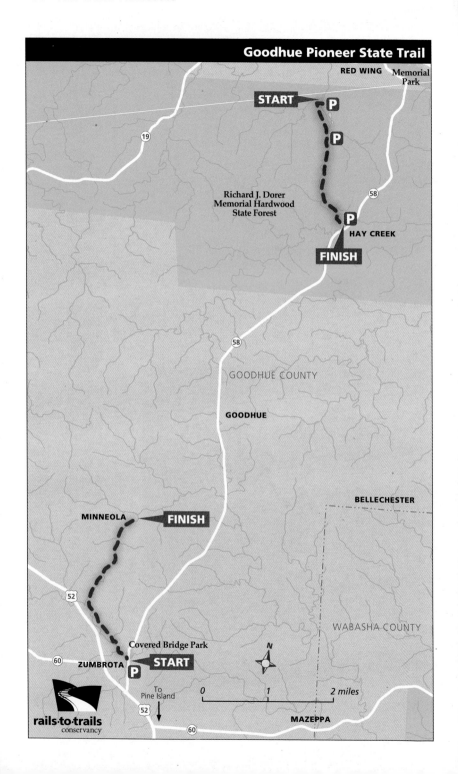

Goodhue Pioneer State Trail

RED WING   Memorial Park

START

19

Richard J. Dorer Memorial Hardwood State Forest

58

HAY CREEK

FINISH

58

GOODHUE COUNTY

GOODHUE

BELLECHESTER

MINNEOLA   FINISH

52

WABASHA COUNTY

Covered Bridge Park

60   ZUMBROTA   START

To Pine Island

52

N

0   1   2 miles

MAZEPPA

60

rails·to·trails
conservancy

This portion of the trail currently ends at the private Hay Creek Valley Campground in Hay Creek Township.

The 5.5-mile southern half begins at Covered Bridge Park in Zumbrota, home to Minnesota's last remaining covered bridge. Less than 2 miles from the southern trailhead, there is another covered bridge over a shallow ravine. This section of trail passes through farmland and prairies before ending north of 410th Street in rural Minneola Township. The trail is popular with snowmobilers in the winter.

In Red Wing, trail users can take a city trail about 2 miles north and several blocks west to reach the eastern trailhead of the popular Cannon Valley Trail.

Future plans connect the trail with the cities of Red Wing, Goodhue, Zumbrota, Mazeppa, Bellechester, and Pine Island (intersecting with the Douglas State Trail) for a distance of 47 miles.

CONTACT: dnr.state.mn.us/state_trails/goodhue_pioneer

DIRECTIONS

To reach a small turnoff parking area in Red Wing, from Saint Paul take US 10/US 61 19.8 miles south. Turn left onto Red Wing Blvd./MN 316. In 9.8 miles turn right onto US 61, and in 11.5 miles turn right onto Bench St. In 1.5 miles turn left onto County Road 66/Pioneer Road, and go 1.4 miles. Turn right onto Hay Creek Trail, and in 1.5 miles reach the small pulloff.

Additional parking is available just inside the entrance to the Hay Creek Unit recreation area of the Richard J. Dorer Memorial Hardwood State Forest. Follow the directions above, but go 3.4 miles on Hay Creek Trail. Turn left into the day-use area to reach the parking lot.

In Zumbrota, park in Covered Bridge Park or at the library. From Saint Paul, take US 52 S., and drive 52 miles south. Turn left onto 445th St., and in 0.2 mile turn right onto Jefferson Ave. In 0.8 mile turn left onto W. Second St. In 0.4 mile turn left onto West Ave. for the library parking. Or go 0.5 mile on W. Second St., and turn left onto Main St. The Covered Bridge Park entrance will be on your left in 0.2 mile.

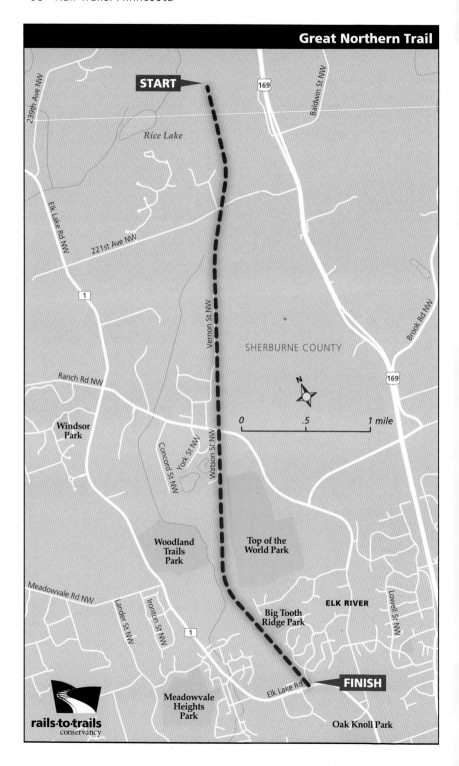

Great Northern Trail

The Great Northern Trail offers a paved north-south route across the city of Elk River on the fringe of the northwestern outskirts of Minneapolis. For nearly 5 miles, the rail-trail winds through the community along a former railroad bed operated by the Great Northern Railroad 1886–1976. Currently, the trail is paved from County Road 1 in the northern section of Elk River to the city limits. A grass-surfaced section continues on to the Zimmerman city line.

Heading north from the residential section of the trail, it travels through lush stands of hardwood forests and several parks, including Big Tooth Ridge Park and Top of the World Park, where unpaved trails are limited to hiking only. The Great Northern Trail then continues on along the east side of the Elk River Golf Club. The

This pleasant corridor through the community of Elk River is a bird-watcher's paradise.

Location
Sherburne

Endpoints
County Road 1/Elk Lake Road N.W. and Upland St. N.W. to 0.9 mile north of 221st Ave. N.W. and 0.4 mile west of US 169 (Elk River)

Mileage
4.6

Type
Rail-Trail

Roughness Index
1, 3

Surface
Asphalt, Grass

trail offers scenic views and includes a pedestrian tunnel under CR 33 (Ranch Road) that provides users with an unimpeded 4.6-mile route through Elk River. Just west of the trail, one can also access Woodland Trails Park, a beautiful natural park featuring dense woods, prairies, and wetlands, all spanning more than 300 acres.

Future plans target developing the rest of the trail from the Elk River city limits to Zimmerman, about 4 miles north on US 169, and then beyond to Princeton, ultimately adding another 8 miles to the trail.

CONTACT: elkrivermn.gov/facilities/facility/details/great-northern-trail-14

DIRECTIONS

To reach the southern terminus of the trail, take I-94 to Exit 207 (if taking I-94 E.) or 207B (if taking I-94 W.). Merge onto MN 101, heading north, and go 6.2 miles (6.9 miles if you took I-94 E.). Exit onto US 10 toward Elk River. Merge onto US 10, and go 1.7 miles west. Turn right onto Proctor Ave. N.W., which becomes Elk Lake Road N.W./County Road 1. In 1.2 miles turn right onto Vernon St. N.W. Parking is available at Meadowvale Elementary School.

Roadside parking and trail access are available just south of Ranch Road N.W. at the intersection of Watson St. N.W. and 208th Ave. N.W. Take I-94 to Exit 207 (if taking I-94 E.) or 207B (if taking I-94 W.). Merge onto MN 101, heading north, and go 6.2 miles (6.9 miles if you took I-94 E.). Continue on US 169 3.3 miles, and take the CR 33 exit. Turn left onto 205th Ave. N.W. (which becomes Ranch Road N.W.), and go 1.1 miles. Turn left onto Watson St. N.W.; trail access is 0.2 mile south on the left.

The Great River Ridge State Trail runs for 13 miles between County Road 9 just north of Eyota and Third Street Southwest just north of Wabasha Street in the town of Plainview, which serves as the agricultural hub of the area. There are plans to extend the trail another 2 miles south into the town of Eyota at the southern terminus. The entire trail is paved, and there is an additional adjacent trail with a natural surface for horseback riders and snow-mobilers between the current southern trailhead at CR 9 and the town of Elgin.

The trail traverses both flat and some hilly terrain through a largely open agriculture-dominated landscape. Wind and sun can be intense at times and few amenities are available along the trail, so it is important to bring plenty of water. In the northern section, the trail parallels

The shelter in downtown Elgin provides a nice respite from the sun.

Location
Olmsted, Wabasha

Endpoints
Third St. S.W. just north of Wabasha St. (Plain-view) to County Road 9 and 0.3 mile west of MN 42 (Eyota)

Mileage
13

Type
Rail-Trail

Roughness Index
1

Surface
Asphalt, Crushed Stone

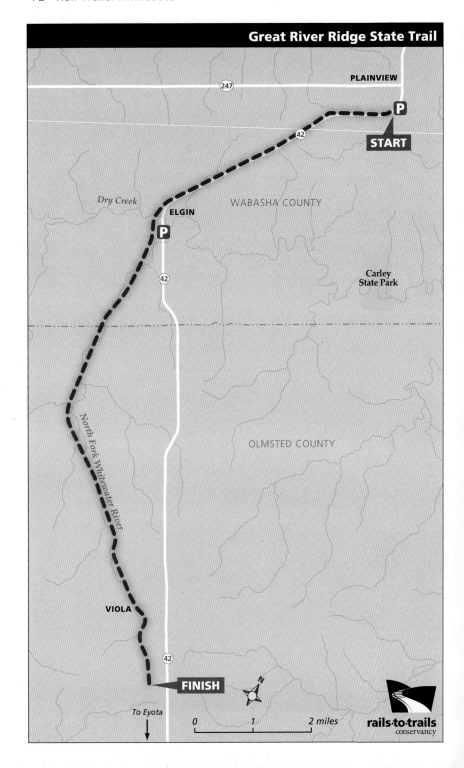

Great River Ridge State Trail

PLAINVIEW

247

42

START

Dry Creek

ELGIN

WABASHA COUNTY

Carley
State Park

42

North Fork Whitewater River

OLMSTED COUNTY

VIOLA

42

FINISH

To Eyota

0   1   2 miles

N

rails·to·trails
conservancy

MN 42 to Elgin, where it begins to head more westerly. From Elgin, the trail passes largely through agricultural landscapes, where some shade is provided along a partially wooded corridor, especially along a section that parallels the North Fork of the Whitewater River as you approach Viola and then southward toward CR 9.

Future development of the trail also includes extending it to Carley State Park, about 4 miles east of Elgin. Carley State Park serves as an overflow campground for Whitewater State Park, a few miles farther to the southeast.

CONTACT: dnr.state.mn.us/state_trails/great_river_ridge

DIRECTIONS

To reach the Plainview trailhead, from Saint Paul, take US 52 S., and go 62.8 miles south to Exit 68. Turn left onto Ash Road N.W., and go 20.9 miles east, as the road changes to White Bridge N.W./County Road 12 and then MN 247. Turn right onto Third St. S.W.; the trailhead and parking are on the right in 0.4 mile.

To reach the southern trailhead outside of Eyota, from Saint Paul, take US 52 S., and go 72.2 miles south to Exit 58. Turn left onto 37th St. N.W., which becomes E. Circle Drive N.E., and go 5.7 miles. Turn left onto Collegeview Road E., which becomes CR 9, and go 8.2 miles. The trailhead is on the left.

There is also a midpoint trailhead/access in downtown Elgin on the south side of Main St. E., between Center Ave. N. and First Ave. N.E. From Saint Paul, take US 52 S., and go 62.8 miles south to Exit 68. Turn left onto Ash Road N.W., and go 15.6 miles east, as the road changes to White Bridge N.W./CR 12 and then MN 247. Turn right onto CR 2, and in 2.4 miles turn left onto Main St. W.; the trailhead and parking are on the right in 0.3 mile.

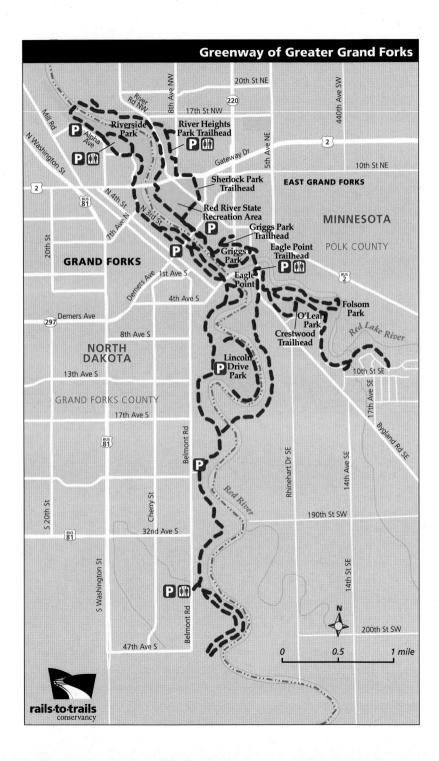

Grand Forks, North Dakota, and East Grand Forks, Minnesota, host a network of paved paths along the Red River and Red Lake River that form the border between these two cities.

At just more than 20 miles, the Greenway of Greater Grand Forks, known as the Greenway, includes a 10-mile loop through both cities that enables bikers/hikers to link up to other trails through each city. In addition, bikers can also access the 100-mile paved route of the Rural Bicycle Loop in Grand Forks, North Dakota.

The Greenway trails developed out of a massive project to mitigate damage from disastrous seasonal flooding on the Red River. The network of trails traverses through a 2,200-acre natural open space along the river in both cities. A unique feature of this system of urban trails is the limited trail crossings for vehicles, thus allowing for long stretches of recreational use.

The cities are linked by two bridges over the river that are designated for nonmotorized use only, making for a

Location
Grand Forks (ND), Polk (MN)

Endpoints
19th St. N.W. and 20th St. N.W. to Eighth St. S.E. and 19th Ave. S.E. (East Grand Forks, MN) and Gateway Drive/US 2 and N. First St. to 14th Ave. N.W. and Loamy Hills Place (Grand Forks, ND)

Mileage
21.1

Type
Greenway/Non-Rail-Trail

Roughness Index
1

Surface
Asphalt

This trail is great for bikers and includes two designated nonmotorized bridges, making this a delightful ride between Minnesota and North Dakota.

delightful ride between the states. Access to facilities abounds along the trail. East Grand Forks in Minnesota has four designated trailheads: at River Heights in the Red River State Recreation Area campground, Griggs Park at the south end of downtown East Grand Forks, at Eagle Point on First Street Southeast at the confluence of the Red and Red Lake Rivers, and Crestwood at O'Leary Park on Fourth Street Southeast. The trail can also be accessed from over 10 locations along its route. There are 14 designated parking areas throughout the Greenway, 11 restrooms, and 10 information kiosks.

Other amenities along the trails include playgrounds, picnic areas, campgrounds, golf courses, shore bank fishing sites, and myriad open spaces. Interpretive historic, wildlife, and geology plaques are located throughout the Greenway system. Wildflowers and animals can be seen along the banks of both rivers that run the entire length of the Greenway. The trail also offers an ideal venue for winter activities, including groomed cross-country ski routes.

CONTACT: greenwayggf.com

DIRECTIONS

There are dozens of places to park to access the various segments of the trail.

To reach trailhead parking with restrooms in North Dakota, take I-29 to Exit 130. Head east on Seventh Ave. N.E., and go 0.4 mile. Take the first left onto 11th St. N.E./S. Columbia Road/County Road 17, which becomes CR 81 and then S. Washington St. Go 6.5 miles, and turn right onto 62nd Ave. S.E. In 0.8 mile turn left onto Belmont Road. In 1.6 miles, just before Belmont Court, you will see the trailhead parking on your right.

To reach parking at Lincoln Drive Park in North Dakota, follow the directions above to Belmont Road. Once on Belmont, go 3.3 miles north, and turn right onto Lincoln Drive and enter the park.

To reach parking at Riverside Park in North Dakota, take I-29 to Exit 141. Head east on Gateway Drive/US 2. In 2 miles turn left onto Mill Road, and go 0.5 mile. Turn right onto Red Dot Place, and in 0.2 mile turn left to access the parking lot.

In Minnesota, parking is available in River Heights Park. Take I-29 to Exit 141 (in North Dakota). Head east on Gateway Drive/US 2, and go 2.7 miles, entering Minnesota, and take the exit for East Grand Forks. Turn left onto Fourth St. N.W./River Road N.W., and parking will be 0.3 mile ahead on the right.

To reach parking just south of the confluence of Red River and Red Lake River in Minnesota, take I-29 to Exit 140 (in North Dakota). Head east on Demers Ave./MN 297, and go 2.4 miles to the Fourth Ave. S. exit. Continue on Fourth Ave. S. 0.6 mile, and turn left onto Minnesota Ave. Go 0.5 mile, entering Minnesota, and turn left into the parking lot just before the Third Ave. bridge.

The Hardwood Creek Regional Trail is actually two parallel trails running along US 61 in rural Washington County. The paved trail is open for biking, walking, running, and in-line skating, while the adjacent grass trail is exclusively for equestrian use in the summer and snowmobile use in the winter. The entirety of the trail is located on a former Burlington Northern Railroad corridor. Resurfaced in the spring of 2015, the entire trail offers a smooth, level, and nearly arrow-straight route between its two trailhead communities.

Begin your journey in Hugo, a bedroom community featuring many shops and restaurants. The views quickly change to open fields as you leave residential areas. Several other places of business can be found in downtown Forest

The trail offers a smooth, level, and nearly arrow-straight route between its two trailhead communities.

Location
Washington

Endpoints
US 61 and 145th St. N.
(Hugo) to US 61 and
240th St. N. (Forest Lake)

Mileage
9.5

Type
Rail-Trail

Roughness Index
1

Surface
Asphalt, Grass

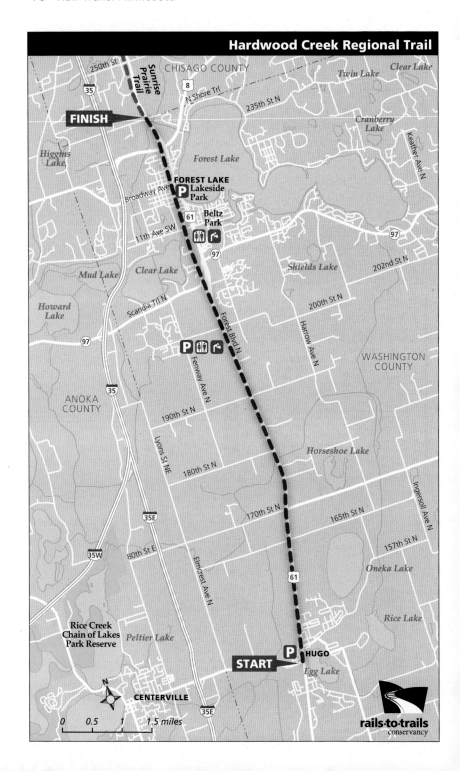

Hardwood Creek Regional Trail

Lake, located just south of the trail's northern endpoint. At the Washington–Chisago county line, the Hardwood Creek Regional Trail becomes the Sunrise Prairie Trail, which continues north for another 17 miles to North Branch. A more practical access point for those wanting to take the trail south from Forest Lake is to start near US 61 and Broadway Avenue. A little more than a mile south of the official northern terminus, this trail access offers ample parking, nearby retail shops and services, and a chance to enjoy Lakeside Park, just two blocks east on the shores of Forest Lake.

CONTACT: co.washington.mn.us/index.aspx?nid=506

DIRECTIONS

To reach the Hugo trailhead, take I-35E N. to Exit 123A. Head east on Main St., which becomes Frenchman Road, and go 1.8 miles. Turn left onto Forest Blvd. N., and in 0.3 mile turn left onto 146th St. N. Parking is on the left.

Parking is also available at the Washington County Headwaters Service and Transit Center located at Headwaters Pkwy. and US 61 near the trail's midpoint. Take I-35 N. to Exit 129. Head east on Lake Drive N.E./MN 97, and go 1.8 miles. Turn right onto Forest Road N., and go 1.2 miles. The transit center is on the left.

In Forest Lake, park at US 61 and Broadway Ave. Take I-35 to Exit 131. Head east 0.8 mile on W. Broadway Ave. Parking is on the left just after crossing US 61.

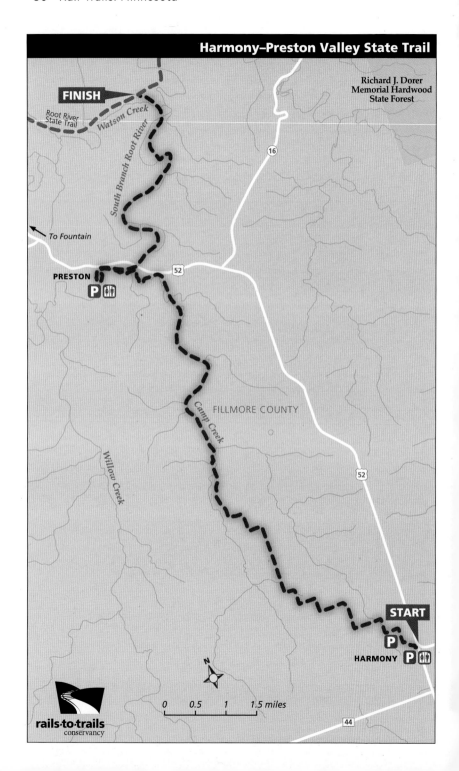

Harmony–Preston Valley State Trail

Richard J. Dorer
Memorial Hardwood
State Forest

FINISH

Root River
State Trail

Watson Creek

South Branch Root River

To Fountain

PRESTON
P 🚻

52

16

Camp Creek

FILLMORE COUNTY

Willow Creek

52

START
P

HARMONY
P 🚻

44

N

0   0.5   1   1.5 miles

rails·to·trails
conservancy

The Harmony–Preston Valley State Trail runs 18 miles on a north-south line between the town of Harmony and the Root River State Trail, which it meets between Lanesboro and Fountain. The paved trail is mostly level, although a section just north of Harmony is relatively steep.

An old railroad right-of-way creates the foundation for the northern two-thirds of the Harmony–Preston Valley State Trail. The northern portion of this section passes through lush woodlands and farmlands as it winds along and across Watson Creek, the South Branch of the Root River, and Camp Creek.

The southern portion begins in Harmony, noted for its rich Amish heritage and green business operations today. The trail leaves the railroad grade and climbs up through some of its most challenging sections as it continues north out of the river bottom to the valley rim, offering broad

Meandering valley streams and creeks help make up the character of this beautiful trail.

Location
Fillmore

Endpoints
Root River State Trail near the intersection of Heron Road and County Road 17 (northeast of Preston) to Harmony Visitor Center at Second St. N.W. near US 52 (Harmony)

Mileage
18

Type
Rail-Trail

Roughness Index
1

Surface
Asphalt

vistas of the surrounding countryside. Just 0.5 mile from Harmony, an interpretive site highlights some of the glacial history of the area.

Settled in 1853 alongside the Root River, Preston's history is that of a southern Minnesota milling town. From Preston, continuing another 5.5 miles north and casually paralleling the South Branch of the Root River, the trail links up with the Root River State Trail just east of Isinours Junction (and a northern trailhead parking option), providing an additional 42 miles of trail network.

The Harmony–Preston Valley State Trail is popular with cyclists, hikers, and in-line skaters; cross-country skiing is popular during winter. Local waters offer some of the best trout fishing in southern Minnesota. Forested hills and meandering valley streams and creeks are all part of the natural character of this trail. Although a lot of wildlife can be observed along this trail, Minnesota's timber rattlesnake is perhaps the most ominous. Though infrequent, they can typically be found among rock outcrops, along river bottoms or even warming themselves right on the trail. The timber rattlesnake is a protected state species and should be respected, along with all wildlife.

Restrooms and parking are available at the trailhead centers in both Preston and Harmony. Both towns also have a bicycle tune-up station located at each trailhead. The trail managers warn users not to leave valuables in their cars while enjoying the trail.

CONTACT: dnr.state.mn.us/state_trails/harmony_preston

DIRECTIONS

In Harmony, there are two places to park: Take I-90 to Exit 218. Turn left onto US 52 S., and go 37.2 miles to Fourth St. N.W. Turn right onto Fourth St. N.W, and go 0.2 mile west to the parking lot on the left.

Alternatively, park at the tourist information center at the end of Second St. N.W. just off Main St. Take I-90 to Exit 218. Turn left onto US 52 S., and go 37.3 miles. Turn right onto Main Ave. N., and immediately turn right onto Second St. N.W. for the tourist information center parking lot.

To the trailhead in Preston, take I-90 to Exit 218. Turn left onto US 52 S., and go 26.8 miles. Turn right onto St. Paul St. N.W., and go 0.3 mile. Turn left onto Fillmore St. Parking will be on the left in 0.2 mile.

Parking is also available at Isinours Junction, about 0.8 mile west of the junction with the Root River State Trail north of Preston. Take I-90 to Exit 218. Turn left onto US 52 S., and go 21.5 miles. Turn left onto County Road 8, and go 4.2 miles. Turn right onto CR 17. In 1.8 miles turn right onto a gravel road. The lot is 0.5 mile down the road. Head east on Root River State Trail, and go 0.8 mile to the junction with Harmony–Preston Valley State Trail. Turn right.

The Heartland State Trail is one of many long-distance trails managed by the Minnesota Department of Natural Resources. When established in 1974, it became one of the first rail-trail conversions in the country. The nearly 50-mile trail connects the small cities of Park Rapids and Cass Lake along a forested route. As you might expect from a trail in the heart of the Land of 10,000 Lakes, the Heartland State Trail runs past a number of lakes, rivers, and streams, many of which are directly accessible from the pathway. Public beaches, resorts, and campgrounds also line the route, so be sure to bring your bathing suit and fishing gear. When water is not the primary vista, towering white pine, spruce fir, and hardwood forests offer shade and habitat for various animals, including raccoons, red foxes, white-tailed deer, beavers, and porcupines.

The trail also skirts the edge of both Paul Bunyan State Forest and Chippewa National Forest, home to a

The shade provided by the trees makes this path more enjoyable on a summer day.

Location
Cass, Hubbard

Endpoints
First St. E./MN 34 just west of Riverside Ave. (Park Rapids) to Aspen Ave./MN 371 and Railroad St. (Cass Lake)

Mileage
49

Type
Rail-Trail

Roughness Index
1

Surface
Asphalt

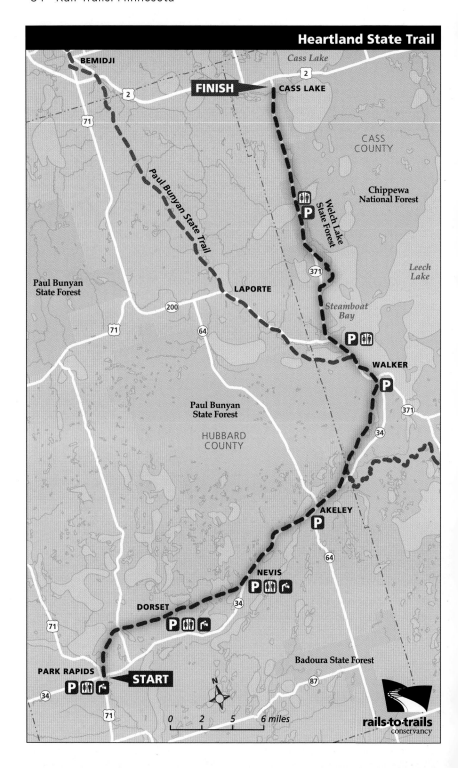

Heartland State Trail

BEMIDJI

Cass Lake

2

FINISH

CASS LAKE

2

71

CASS
COUNTY

Paul Bunyan State Trail

Chippewa
National Forest

Welch Lake
State Forest

P

Paul Bunyan
State Forest

LAPORTE

200

Leech
Lake

371

Steamboat
Bay

71

64

P

WALKER

P

Paul Bunyan
State Forest

371

HUBBARD
COUNTY

34

AKELEY

P

64

NEVIS

P

DORSET

P

34

PARK RAPIDS

P

START

Badoura State Forest

34

71

87

N

0   2   5   6 miles

rails·to·trails
conservancy

large population of bald eagles. Because the Heartland State Trail is a rail-trail, the trek is fairly level and smooth. Still, those desiring a rest will want to stop in Dorset, Akeley, or Nevis, three small resort towns hosting restaurants and shops. Just west of the city of Walker on Leech Lake, indefatigable trail users can connect directly to the even longer Paul Bunyan State Trail. The Heartland State Trail resumes again where it crosses Morris Point Road at the west side of Walker Bay on Leech Lake.

An adjacent grass path between Park Rapids and Walker accommodates both equestrian users and mountain bikers, while a parallel treadway for snowmobilers runs from Walker to Cass Lake. Just north of Walker, a 4-mile segment of the trail leaves the level former railroad corridor, so be forewarned: The terrain here becomes significantly hillier.

About 2.5 miles south of Cass Lake, the trail crosses MN 371 at 148th Street Northwest (Pike Bay Loop Road/County Road 76), where it links up with the 19-mile, paved Mi-Gi-Zi Trail around Pike Bay. An alternate route at 148th Street Northwest is to continue north along the east side of MN 371 into Cass Lake and follow the streets up around to the northwest corner of the city, where Second Street Northeast/CR 206 swings north to meet US 2; there is a full-service rest stop here on the north side of the highway. Parking is also available on the south side of US 2.

CONTACT: dnr.state.mn.us/state_trails/heartland

DIRECTIONS

A medium-size parking lot is available in Heartland County Park at the trail's southern endpoint in Park Rapids, where the trail meets Mill St. From the intersection of MN 210 and MN 371 in Baxter, near Brainerd, head west on MN 210. Go 19.5 miles, and turn right onto US 10. In 18.2 miles turn right onto N.W. Brown St./County Road 23. In 16 miles turn left onto MN 227, and in 0.3 mile turn right onto Hubbard Road/CR 23, which becomes CR 6. In 14.8 miles turn left onto CR 6/MN 87. In 5.3 miles turn left onto MN 34/First St. E. In 0.7 mile turn right onto Mill St., and then make a slight left onto Heartland St. in 0.4 mile. Parking is straight ahead within Heartland County Park.

Small parking lots are also available in Dorset, Nevis, Akeley, Walker, Erickson's Landing, and Cass Lake.

Parking and restrooms are available at Steamboat Lake landing. From the intersection of MN 210 and MN 371 in Baxter, near Brainerd, head north on MN 371. Go 54.3 miles, and turn left onto MN 371/MN 200; continue another 18 miles. Turn left onto CR 141, and in 0.1 mile turn left to reach the parking lot.

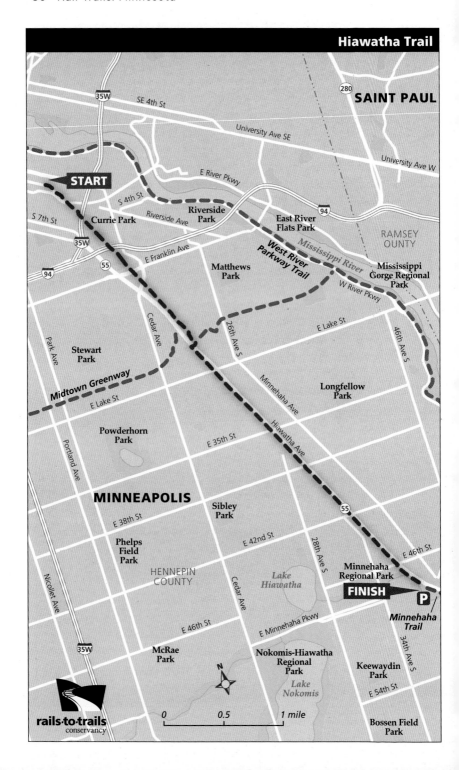

Hiawatha Trail

Minnesota's Hiawatha Trail (also known as the Hiawatha LRT Trail) runs along a north-south route paralleling both Hiawatha Avenue and the Metro Transit Blue Line in Minneapolis. The trail connects downtown Minneapolis and the vibrant Cedar-Riverside neighborhood in the north to Minnehaha Creek, Minnehaha Park, and the former site of the Longfellow Zoological Gardens in the south.

The trail begins just one block north of the site of the former Metrodome (demolished in 2014) at Norm McGrew Place and South Third Street in the Downtown East neighborhood. Bike lanes along South Third Street and South Fourth Street (as well as an extension from Chicago Avenue) allow for a trek deeper into the heart of Minneapolis. Upon completion of the new Vikings stadium, access, lane routes, and area parking may affect this downtown trailhead.

This trail offers key connections and intersects the Midtown Greenway, providing more vehicle-free distance for cycling.

Location
Hennepin

Endpoints
Norm McGrew Place/
Ninth Ave. and S. Third
St. to E. Minnehaha
Pkwy. and Hiawatha Ave.
(Minneapolis)

Mileage
4.7

Type
Rail-with-Trail

Roughness Index
1

Surface
Asphalt, Concrete

Continuing south from the former Metrodome site, the Hiawatha Trail crosses busy I-35 West on the light rail overpass and under I-94 just north of the large Metro Transit storage and maintenance facility. The trail cuts through a portion of the Cedar-Riverside neighborhood as it continues southward, finally getting into a more residential setting once it crosses Franklin Avenue. At East 24th Street, a bicycle and pedestrian bridge over Hiawatha Avenue/MN 55 carries trail users to the Phillips community of Minneapolis.

Just past East 26th Street, the stunning Martin Olav Sabo Bridge connects the Hiawatha Trail with the popular Midtown Greenway over Hiawatha Avenue. Those wishing to continue south on the Hiawatha Trail should cross to the western side of the road, where the trail surface changes from asphalt to concrete. The section of trail from East 28th Street south to East 32nd Street is little more than a sidewalk; trail users should exercise caution when navigating this section. Fortunately, Minneapolis has targeted this portion of the Hiawatha Trail for improvement in the future.

For most of the rest of its route, the trail is wedged between the light rail line and Hiawatha Avenue. The light rail station and platforms at 38th Street and 46th Street each have Nice Ride bike rental stations. At East 46th Street, trail users cross the tracks and pick up the trail on the western side of the Metro Transit Blue Line as it continues running parallel to MN 55/Hiawatha Avenue.

After just one block, the trail ends at Minnehaha Parkway in the Minnehaha neighborhood, where a short walk, run, or bike along the road leads to the appropriately named Minnehaha Trail.

Both the Hiawatha and West River Parkway Trails link the Minnehaha Park area with the eastern side of downtown Minneapolis. The Hiawatha Trail offers a fast, direct, no-frills pathway alongside high-traffic streets and railroad tracks just south of downtown.

CONTACT: metrobiketrails.weebly.com/hennepin-county.html#hiawatha

DIRECTIONS

From I-35W, take Exit 13. Head east on E. 46th St., and go 1.4 miles. Turn right onto Cedar Ave., and go 0.3 mile. Turn left onto E. Minnehaha Pkwy., and go 1.6 miles. Turn right into the parking lot.

Parking can be found in the southern residential section once E. Minnehaha Pkwy. crosses over Hiawatha Ave. There is also metered street parking along S. Minnehaha Drive at Minnehaha Falls, in addition to a number of parking lots in downtown Minneapolis. Parking is also available along neighborhood streets that intersect with the trail south of Franklin Ave. to the end of the trail.

Until it became inactive in 1948, visitors used a rail spur to come to Taylors Falls from Minneapolis and Saint Paul to find relaxation, enjoy recreation, and see the rare Glacial Gardens of Interstate State Park.

Today, the former rail corridor hosts a small trail network—the Interstate State Park to Taylors Falls Trail—comprising two trails that run briefly along either side of the St. Croix, Minnesota's only designated National Wild and Scenic River. One trail segment, the Railroad Trail, runs 1.5 miles on the northwest side of US 8/MN 95, somewhat removed from the river and among a densely forested canopy.

The 1.25-mile River Trail follows along the steep, forested slopes high above the river on the southeast side of US 8/MN 95. Together, they form a trail loop that can be

Three overlooks along the River Trail feature vistas of the St. Croix River.

Location
Chisago

Endpoints
Milltown Road and MN 95/US 8 in Interstate State Park to Bench St. and MN 95/US 8 (Taylors Falls)

Mileage
2.75

Type
Rail-Trail

Roughness Index
2–3

Surface
Dirt, Grass

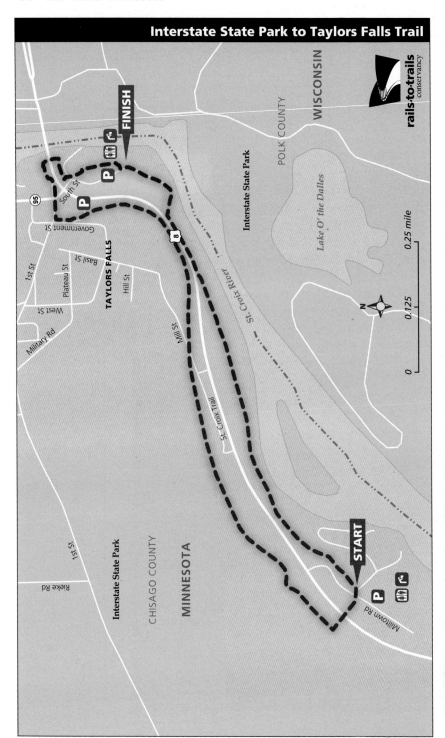

Interstate State Park to Taylors Falls Trail

accessed at either end of the parking lot at Taylors Falls past the boat rental area in the state park parking lot or from near the park headquarters in the southern state park unit on Milltown Road.

Both routes are fairly level but have steep stairways along segments of each trail. The trails can be taken independently or can be started at either end to create a 2.75-mile loop route that goes along the beautiful St. Croix River and through a dense corridor of Minnesota hardwoods. The north end of both the Railroad Trail and River Trail are linked by a short two-block segment along city streets (Government Street and First Street) and a pedestrian river walkway.

Trail users can snowshoe and cross-country ski on the railroad section of the trail during winter, but the river section of the trail would provide a challenge for snowshoers and would be too rough for cross-country skiing. Other park activities include climbing the bluffs along the river, flat-water canoeing, kayaking in the rapids, and taking an excursion by tour boat. During spring the park is alive with wildflowers, and during fall the forests turn brilliant colors. You can also see 10 different kinds of lava flow that are exposed in the park as well as glacial potholes and other geological features.

Future development associated with the trail includes the Swedish Immigrant Trail Project that will connect the cities of Taylors Falls, Shafer, Center City, Lindstrom, Chisago City, and Wyoming in southern Chisago County with a multiuse trail.

CONTACT: dnr.state.mn.us/state_parks/interstate

DIRECTIONS

Interstate State Park is approximately 45 miles northeast of Minneapolis/Saint Paul on US 8. Parking and restrooms are available at both Taylors Falls and in the southern unit of Interstate State Park.

To reach Interstate State Park, take I-35 N. to Exit 132 (there is no exit from I-35 S.). Head east on US 8, and go 20.7 miles. Turn right onto Milltown Road into the park.

To reach parking at the north trailhead, take I-35 N. to Exit 132 (there is no exit from I-35 S.). Head east on US 8, and go 21.7 miles. Turn right onto South St. to access the parking lot.

Lake Minnetonka LRT Regional Trail

rails-to-trails
conservancy

START

169
7

Big Willow Park

Minnesota River Bluffs LRT Regional Trail

169

494

Bryant Lake Regional Park

Bryant Lake

62

HOPKINS

P

494

Jidana Park

McKenzie Park

DEEPHAVEN

MINNETONKA

7

Birch Island Park

Edenvale Park

EDEN PRAIRIE

212

Staring Lake

Staring Lake Park

Red Rock Lake

Miller Park

5

WOODLAND

101

Round Lake

CHANHASSEN

212

101

Carson Bay

GREENWOOD

P

EXCELSIOR

101

Lotus Lake

N

0   1   2 miles

MINNETONKA BEACH

Big Island Nature Park

TONKA BAY

SHOREWOOD

7

Freeman Park

41

Cathcart Park

Lake Minnewashta Regional Park

Lake Minnewashta

CARVER COUNTY

5

41

Dakota Regional Rail Trail

12

ORONO

Luce Line Trail

SPRING PARK

MOUND

Langdon Lake

Lake Minnetonka

HENNEPIN COUNTY

Lake Virginia

Tamarack Lake

VICTORIA

P   Lions Park

Dutch Lake

Stone Lake

Lake Zumbra

Steiger Lake

FINISH

Carver Park Reserve

7

5

The Lake Minnetonka LRT Regional Trail begins in the vicinity of Eighth Avenue North in downtown Hopkins, just a few blocks north of the eastern endpoint of the Minnesota River Bluffs LRT Regional Trail. Currently, there is only a short paved section (from Eighth to 11th Avenues) in the entire 15-mile trail that skirts the edge of Lake Minnetonka on its run through the communities of Minnetonka, Excelsior, and Victoria.

The trail cuts diagonally northwest across residential neighborhoods in the Minneapolis suburb of Hopkins before turning due west at Minnetonka Boulevard. Paralleling the road for about 2 miles, the trail passes under busy I-494. Construction of a light rail segment from 11th Avenue northwest to Shady Oak Road, scheduled for completion in the next three to four years, will include paving that section of the trail as well. From Shady Oak Road to the western trailhead in Victoria, the trail will remain hard-packed crushed gravel as it is for the entire route now.

Though it only joins the trail for a short while, Lake Minnetonka offers stunning views for trail users.

Location
Carver, Hennepin

Endpoints
Eighth Ave. N. just south of First St. N. (Hopkins) to 81st St. west of MN 5/Arboretum Blvd. (Victoria)

Mileage
15

Type
Rail-with-Trail

Roughness Index
2

Surface
Crushed Stone

In the city of Minnetonka, the landscape changes to dense forest, although housing developments are never far away. The trail runs directly behind the large campus of Minnetonka's Middle School East and provides a safe route to school for a number of students.

About halfway into the trek, the trail rejoins Minnetonka Boulevard to cross the Carson Bay inlet of Lake Minnetonka; be sure to stop nearby to check out the stunning views. The trail skirts the shoreline for a short while before passing the former site of the famous Excelsior Amusement Park and entering the city's downtown area. The small city is a great place to stop for a bite to eat.

The rest of the journey to Victoria takes you through a now-familiar mixture of local residential properties and dense woodlands. Victoria is home to the large Carver Park Reserve, which includes horse trails, hiking trails, and a nature center. The park is accessible directly from the Lake Minnetonka LRT Regional Trail on the eastern side of Steiger Lake, just west of the intersection at Park Drive.

CONTACT: threeriversparks.org/trails/lake-minnetonka-trail.aspx

DIRECTIONS

To start in Hopkins, park at the lot at the intersection of Eighth Ave. and Excelsior Blvd. Take I-394 to Exit 3, and follow US 169 4.2 miles south. Take the Excelsior Blvd./County Road 3 exit. Turn right onto Excelsior Blvd. and go 0.3 mile to Eighth Ave. S., where a lot is located. Take Eighth Ave. north a few blocks to reach the trail.

To start in Victoria (west end), take I-494 to Exit 11C. Merge onto US 12, and head 1.2 miles west. Take the MN 5/Arboretum Blvd. exit. Follow MN 5/Arboretum Blvd./W. 78th St. 9.6 miles, and turn right onto Steiger Lake Lane. Park off Steiger Lake Lane in the downtown area.

Parking is also available in Carver Park Reserve. Immediately after turning onto Steiger Lake Lane, turn right to reach parking by the lake.

Another option for parking is in Minnetonka. From I-494, take Exit 17 for Minnetonka Blvd. If coming from I-494 S., turn left onto McGinty Road W., and then turn right onto Minnetonka Blvd. in 0.1 mile. If coming from I-494 N., simply turn right onto Minnetonka Blvd. Head west on Minnetonka Blvd. 0.5 mile. Turn left onto Williston Road, and take an immediate left onto Minnetonka Drive. Parking will be on the left in 0.1 mile.

As fans of public radio can tell you, this trail's name-sake is the fictional town of Lake Wobegon, made famous by author and radio personality Garrison Keillor of *A Prairie Home Companion*. Along the 10-foot-wide paved trail, you'll find small towns that provided Keillor with inspiration, including Holdingford, a town once referred to by Keillor as "most Wobegonic" and which now advertises itself as "The Gateway to Lake Wobegon." Keillor helped dedicate the trail upon its opening in 1998, and he even composed a song for the occasion, appropriately titled "Lake Wobegon Trail."

The trail rests on an inactive Burlington Northern Railroad corridor between the cities of Osakis and St. Joseph. Along the path, which is dotted by trailheads and parking access areas, trail users are treated to scenic views of prairie remnants, lakes, woodlands, and open farmland.

This covered shed was rebuilt from the old Soo Line Railroad Bridge in Holdingford.

Location
Stearns, Todd

Endpoints
First Ave. E. and Main St. at Central Lakes State Trail (Osakis) to 12th Ave. N.E. and County Road 75 (St. Joseph); trail extension: Railroad Ave. west of 13th St. (Albany) to 450th St., 0.8 mile east of 100th Ave. (Holdingford)

Mileage
60

Type
Rail-Trail

Roughness Index
1

Surface
Asphalt

Lake Wobegon Trail

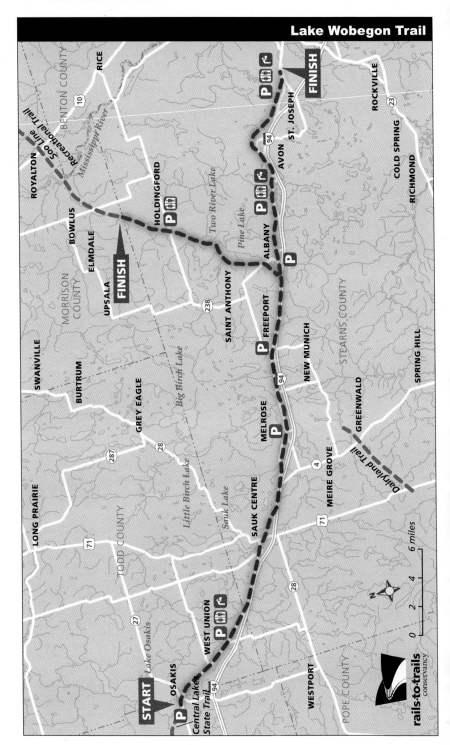

In fact, Stearns County is the top dairy producer in Minnesota. Much of the trail parallels busy I-94, making it a safe alternative for nonmotorized travel in the heart of Minnesota.

Not far from the Avon trailhead is St. John's University, situated on more than 2,000 wooded acres that hold hiking trails and lakes. An extension of the Lake Wobegon Trail north from the city of Albany takes trail users to Holdingford, which features the longest covered bridge in Minnesota.

Beyond Holdingford, the rail-trail continues even farther north to the Stearns–Morrison county line at 450th Street, adding another 13 miles of paved trail with this northern extension. Here, the Soo Line Recreational Trail begins, offering an additional 10.5 miles of paved trail to US 10 just north of Royalton. Ultimately, intrepid recreationists can travel uninterrupted on off-road trails north all the way to Duluth, a distance of more than 150 miles.

This is not the only trail connection provided. The Lake Wobegon Trail's western end in Osakis offers a seamless connection to the 55-mile Central Lakes State Trail. These combined trails give users 115 miles of uninterrupted pavement from St. Joseph to Fergus Falls.

In the near future, the Dairyland Trail will take bikers, walkers, and snowmobilers south from Albany to Brooten. In the east, a planned 7-mile rail-with-trail extension will eventually bring the Lake Wobegon Trail to St. Cloud on the Mississippi River.

CONTACT: lakewobegontrails.com

DIRECTIONS

The trail parallels I-94/US 52 for its entire length. To reach the western trailhead in Osakis, take I-94 E. to Exit 114 for County Road 3/MN 127 (Osakis/Westport). Head northeast on MN 27, and in 1.7 miles turn left onto First Ave. E. In 0.7 mile turn left onto Main St. and find parking along the street.

For the eastern trailhead in St. Joseph, take I-94 to Exit 160. Head northeast on CR 2, and go 1 mile. Turn right onto CR 75, and go 0.9 mile. Turn left onto College Ave. N., and in 0.1 mile turn right onto Elm St. E. Parking will be on the left.

Additional parking and other amenities can also be found in most towns along the trail's route, including in Albany for the northern trail extension.

For parking along the trail extension in Holdingford, take I-94 to Exit 153. Head north on CR 9/Fourth St./Avon Ave. S., and go 9.5 miles. Turn left onto River St. In 0.2 mile the parking lot will be on the right.

For parking in Albany, take I-94 to Exit 147. Head north on Eighth St., and go 0.2 mile. Turn right onto Railroad Ave. In 0.2 mile turn right onto Fifth St. and reach parking along the trail. Follow the trail 1.1 miles west to reach the beginning of the trail extension to Holdingford.

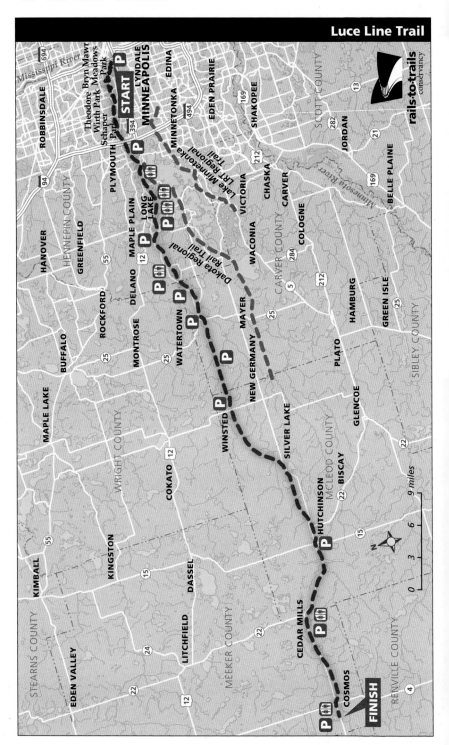

The Luce Line Trail occupies the former railbed of the Electric Short Line Railroad, started in 1908. The tracks continued to be expanded into the late 1920s, when the rail line became known as the Minnesota Western. Passenger service stopped in 1947, and in 1956 the Minneapolis and Saint Louis Railway took over. The corridor became inactive by 1970, and the Luce Line Trail was born. Today, the former railroad corridor accommodates biking, hiking, horseback riding, mountain biking, snowmobiling, and cross-country skiing.

The 9-mile section of paved trail between Theodore Wirth Regional Park and Plymouth and Golden Valley in the western suburbs of Minneapolis is part of the Three Rivers Park District trail system, and that segment is designated as the Luce Line "Regional" Trail. Along the route, Medicine Lake forms the backdrop to wooden bridges that overlook the Bassett Creek marshlands.

It's not surprising that this section of trail is near Cosmos, named for the Greek word that means order and harmony.

Location
Carver, Hennepin, McLeod, Meeker

Endpoints
Bryn Mawr Meadows Park at Van White Memorial Blvd. and I-394 (Minneapolis) to Thompson Lake near MN 7 (Cosmos)

Mileage
72.6

Type
Rail-with-Trail

Roughness Index
1–3

Surface
Asphalt, Crushed Stone, Grass

As trail users enter Theodore Wirth Regional Park, the path becomes part of the Minneapolis Grand Rounds Scenic Byway trail network, and the view expands to include the skyline of downtown Minneapolis. Nearby connections, just west of I-394 and Bryn Mawr Meadows Park, link to several Minneapolis trails, including the Cedar Lake Trail and Midtown Greenway. This section of the Luce Line Trail is routed along the old Bassett's Creek Trail but, as of 2012, is included in the Luce Line Trail system.

The Luce Line Trail leads from urban Minneapolis west through Minnesota's rural landscape, traveling through suburbs and wooded stretches, across wetlands, near lakes, through tallgrass prairie remnants, and into the countryside over varying surfaces. Between Plymouth and Winsted, the trail has a limestone surface with a parallel treadway for equestrians. Between Winsted and Hutchinson, the trail is paved for about 19 miles; between Hutchinson and Cedar Mills it is crushed granite; and between Cedar Mills and Cosmos you'll find mowed grass. Snowmobiles are allowed on the trail west of Stubb's Bay Road in Maple Plain.

Certain areas are not maintained regularly and can be a challenge following instances of severe weather, when the surface becomes muddy or otherwise impassable. Wildlife encountered along the way may include deer, foxes, minks, owls, pheasants, and many species of duck and geese. From Hutchinson westward, the Big Woods eastern forests give way to remnants of the tallgrass prairie, with many prairie plants still visible along the trail.

CONTACT: dnr.state.mn.us/state_trails/luce_line

DIRECTIONS

To reach the eastern endpoint at Bryn Mawr Meadows Park: From I-394 take Exit 7 for Hennepin County Road 2/Penn Ave. Head north on Penn Ave., and immediately turn right onto Oliver Ave. In 0.1 mile turn right again onto Morgan Ave. S. In 0.3 mile turn right into the park.

To begin at Schaper Park, near the eastern endpoint outside of Minneapolis: From I-94 W., take Exit 230 for MN 55 toward Olson Memorial Hwy./Seventh St. N. (There is no Exit 230 from I-94 E.) Turn left onto MN 55 W.; after 2.7 miles, turn right onto Schaper Road, where parking is available in Schaper Park.

To reach the western trailhead in Cosmos, from I-494, take Exit 16B. Head west on MN 7, and go 65.5 miles. Turn right onto 525th Ave. and then left again on 525th Ave. Look for parking ahead to your right.

Parking is also available in the following communities: Plymouth, off 10th Ave. and Vicksburg Lane; Long Lake, off Stubb's Bay Road; Lyndale, off CR 92; Carver, off CR 127, south of CR 20; and in Watertown, Winsted, and Hutchinson.

Running through the colorful heart of northern Minnesota's Iron Range region, the Mesabi Trail is well on its way to becoming one of the longer paved trails in the United States. When completed, the trail will run for 145 miles between Grand Rapids and Ely. Presently, 75 miles are paved between Grand Rapids and McKinley. A trail spur at Gilbert goes to Eveleth, while the main trail continues on to Wynne Lake.

The Mesabi Trail provides the opportunity to connect with nature as the trail winds through woods, stream areas, ponds, and lakes.

Animal sightings on the trail are common, with deer, raccoons, beavers, eagles, hawks, and even black bears making relatively regular appearances. For history buffs, the trail provides an open window to the past and present mining of the Iron Range as it takes users past constructed mine-pit lakes, old iron ore pits, and still-working iron ore mines.

Exposed rock walls are a feature of the Pike River Cut between Virginia and Gilbert.

Location
Itasca, St. Louis

Endpoints
Itasca County Fairgrounds at N.E. 14th St. and Crystal Lake Blvd. (Grand Rapids) to Fayal Road and US 53 (Eveleth) and Wynne Creek Drive and Giants Ridge Road (Biwabik)

Mileage
115

Type
Rail-Trail

Roughness Index
1–2

Surface
Asphalt, Crushed Stone, Gravel

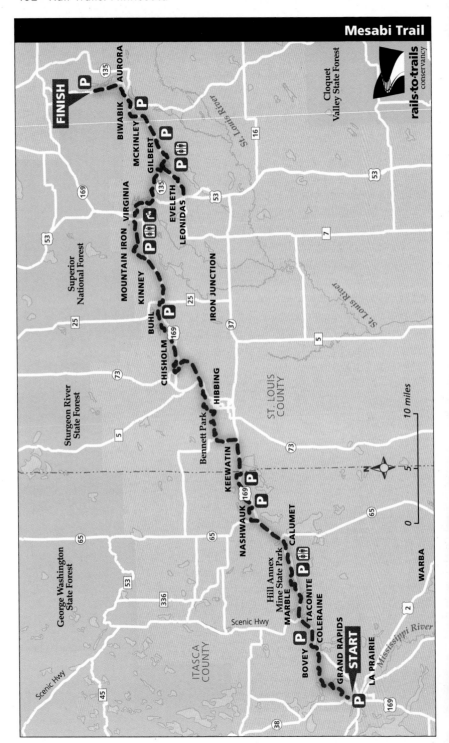

Mesabi Trail

rails-to-trails
conservancy

Cloquet
Valley
State Forest

Superior
National Forest

Sturgeon River
State Forest

George Washington
State Forest

St. Louis River

St. Louis River

ST. LOUIS
COUNTY

ITASCA
COUNTY

Mississippi River

FINISH

AURORA

BIWABIK

MCKINLEY

GILBERT

VIRGINIA

MOUNTAIN IRON

KINNEY

BUHL

CHISHOLM

HIBBING

Bennett Park

KEEWATIN

NASHWAUK

CALUMET

Hill Annex
Mine State Park

MARBLE

TACONITE

COLERAINE

BOVEY

GRAND RAPIDS

START

LA PRAIRIE

WARBA

EVELETH

LEONIDAS

IRON JUNCTION

Scenic Hwy

Scenic Hwy

N

10 miles

5

0

Because the trail connects with so many towns and tourist attractions, such as the United States Hockey Hall of Fame Museum in Eveleth, Hill Annex Mine State Park near Calumet, and the Forest History Center in Grand Rapids, the Mesabi Trail is also viewed as a way to get from place to place without using a car. All the trail routing through communities is along city streets.

A 6-mile section between McKinley and Biwabik is the next section of the trail to be developed in the near future. Also, because of reconstruction work on US 53, scheduled for completion sometime in 2017, the trail between Virginia and Gilbert detours at Mountain Iron and reconnects with the trail in Eveleth.

CONTACT: mesabitrail.com

DIRECTIONS

The western trailhead for the paved section beginning in Grand Rapids is at the Itasca County Fairgrounds (N.W. 14th St. and Crystal Lake Blvd.). Take I-35 to Exit 214, and head west on MN 73. In 2.5 miles turn left onto MN 27/MN 73, and in 4.8 miles, continue straight on MN 73. Go another 35.4 miles, and turn left onto US 2. Travel 36.8 miles, and turn left onto N.E. Fourth St. In 0.2 mile turn right onto N.E. Third Ave., and go 0.7 mile. Turn left onto N.E. 12th St., and then turn right onto Crystal Lake Blvd. In 0.2 mile turn left onto N.E. 14th St., and immediately turn right onto a dirt road. The parking is at the end of the road next to the trail.

In McKinley the paved trailhead and parking lot is on the southwest corner of the intersection of MN 135 and County Road 20. Take I-35 to Exit 237. Continue north 18.9 miles on MN 33. Exit onto US 53, and go 35.9 miles north. Take the MN 37 exit, and turn right onto MN 37. In 2.8 miles turn right onto CR 20/Heritage Trail, where the parking is located.

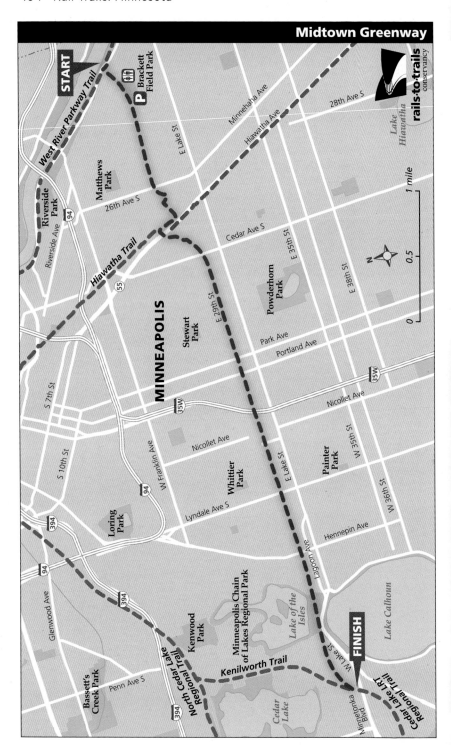

Midtown Greenway

rails-to-trails
conservancy

START

West River Parkway Trail

Brackett Field Park

P

Minnehaha Ave

Hiawatha Ave

28th Ave S

Lake Hiawatha

E Lake St

Matthews Park

26th Ave S

Riverside Park

94

Riverside Ave S

Hiawatha Trail

Cedar Ave S

E 35th St

55

Powderhorn Park

E 38th St

N

1 mile

0.5

0

MINNEAPOLIS

Stewart Park

E 29th St

Park Ave

Portland Ave

S 7th St

35W

35W

Nicollet Ave

S 10th St

W Franklin Ave

Nicollet Ave

94

Whittier Park

E Lake St

Painter Park

W 35th St

Lyndale Ave S

W 36th St

394

Loring Park

Hennepin Ave

94

Lagoon Ave

Lake Calhoun

Glenwood Ave

394

Kenwood Park

Minneapolis Chain of Lakes Regional Park

Lake of the Isles

FINISH

North Cedar Lake Regional Trail

Kenilworth Trail

W Lake St

Cedar Lake LRT Regional Trail

Bassett's Creek Park

Penn Ave S

394

Cedar Lake

Minnetonka Blvd

The 5.5-mile Midtown Greenway follows a former railroad corridor through the heart of south Minneapolis, heading due west from the Mississippi River to the neighborhood of West Calhoun in the scenic Chain of Lakes area. The paved pathway is only one block north of the improving Lake Street corridor and runs parallel to the road for most of its route, thus providing a safe alternative for cyclists and pedestrians to travel instead of the busy street.

Much of the trail is below grade because of a 1912 mandate by the Minneapolis City Council for the Milwaukee Road to dig a trench for its rail line. Presently, the decision ensures that trail users have minimal contact with vehicular traffic. East of MN 55/Hiawatha Avenue, the Minnesota Commercial Railway operates trains on the corridor to this day.

One of the most dramatic features of the trail is the Martin Olav Sabo Bridge.

Location
Hennepin

Endpoints
W. River Pkwy. and E. 27th St. to Kenilworth Trail and Cedar Lake LRT Regional Trail north of W. Lake St. (Minneapolis)

Mileage
5.5

Type
Rail-with-Trail

Roughness Index
1

Surface
Asphalt

This section of the Midtown Greenway is an example of a successful rail-with-trail project. Busy Hiawatha Avenue is crossed via the stunning Martin Olav Sabo Bridge, which is exclusively for bicycle and pedestrian use. Just east of the bridge, trail users can pick up the Hiawatha Trail to travel north to downtown Minneapolis or south to Minnehaha.

On its western end, the Midtown Greenway connects directly to the Cedar Lake LRT Regional Trail, which links Minneapolis to the suburbs of St. Louis Park, Hopkins, and beyond via other connecting trails. Traveling north on the Kenilworth Trail—also located at the Midtown Greenway's western end—leads trail users to the longer North Cedar Lake Regional Trail. East of Hiawatha Avenue, a short segment of the trail is above ground; to the west through much of south Minneapolis, it runs below street level.

In the east, bicyclists and pedestrians can join the West River Parkway Trail for a longer ride, run, or walk along the Mississippi River. Just a few blocks east of the intersection with the West River Parkway, a ramp at Brackett Field Park lets users access/exit the trail. There is ample parking on nearby streets.

In the future, a streetcar line may be installed in the Midtown Greenway corridor, although a separated trail would still be maintained. There has also been local interest in extending the trail east over the Mississippi River into the Prospect Park neighborhood of Minneapolis and onward into Saint Paul.

The Midtown Greenway connects to the West River Parkway Trail, which users can take south to Minnehaha Regional Park or north to other trail intersections heading into downtown or across the river to the University of Minnesota.

CONTACT: midtowngreenway.org

DIRECTIONS

To access parking at Brackett Field Park, take I-94 E. to Exit 235A toward Riverside Ave./25th Ave. Merge onto S. Ninth St., and then immediately turn right onto 26th Ave. S. In 0.5 mile turn left onto E. 25th St., and in another 0.7 mile turn right onto 36th Ave. S. Go 0.4 mile to E. 28th St., and in 0.2 mile turn left onto S. 39th Ave. to reach Brackett Field Park. The trail has multiple access points throughout downtown.

Minnehaha Trail connects two popular parks in the Twin Cities as it follows the course of the Mississippi River through a corridor that is a mix of woodland and open areas.

At the trail's southern end, in Saint Paul, is Fort Snelling State Park, which offers many recreational opportunities, including canoeing, swimming, and fishing, as well as trails for hiking, biking, and cross-country skiing. At the trail's northern end, in Minneapolis, is the 53-foot Minnehaha Falls, one of the city's most stunning, must-see natural features. The surrounding Minnehaha Regional Park is also beautiful, with limestone bluffs and river overlooks.

The northern end of the Minnehaha Trail is within blocks of three major trails: the Grand Rounds Scenic Byway System that encircles the Twin Cities and includes two trails that head into the heart of downtown; the Hiawatha Trail's southern trailhead, which is just two

The trail runs through the wooded Mississippi River corridor between Minnehaha Falls and Fort Snelling State Park.

Location
Hennepin

Endpoints
Post Road and MN 5 in Fort Snelling State Park (Saint Paul) to S. Minnehaha Drive and E. Minnehaha Pkwy. at Minnehaha Regional Park (Minneapolis)

Mileage
5

Type
Rail-Trail

Roughness Index
1

Surface
Asphalt

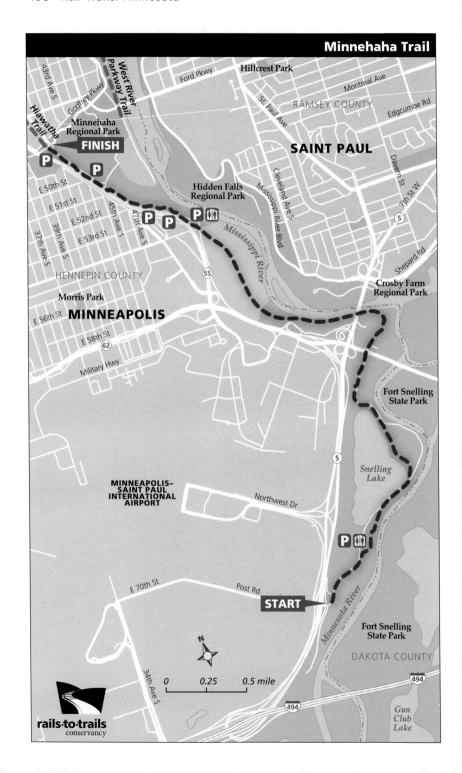

Minnehaha Trail

blocks to the west along Minnehaha Parkway; and the West River Parkway's southern terminus, which begins at the eastern end of Godfrey Parkway/West River Parkway and skirts along the northern boundary of Minnehaha Falls for a few blocks to the entrance to Lock and Dam No. 1 (small parking lot) on the Mississippi River.

As the trail exits Minnehaha Falls, it follows a wooded corridor along the bluff line above the Mississippi River, offering frequent views of the channel below. It comes into Fort Snelling State Park just north of the visitor center and blends into the Snelling Lake Trail, one of many trails that weave through the park. The Minnehaha Trail ends at the park's south entrance.

Yet another trail spur at the south end of the Minnehaha Regional Park segment of the trail crosses the MN 55 bridge into Mendota, where trail users can pick up the Big Rivers Regional Trail.

Two Nice Ride bike-rental stations are located along this trail: one near the Coldwater Spring section of the trail at Minnehaha Falls and one at the visitor center in Fort Snelling State Park.

CONTACT: **metrobiketrails.weebly.com/hennepin-county.html#minnehaha2**

DIRECTIONS

To reach southern parking near Fort Snelling State Park, take I-94 to Exit 237. Head south on Cretin Ave. N., and go 2.5 miles. Turn left onto W. Highland Pkwy., and in 0.3 mile turn right onto Cleveland Ave. S. Go 1.4 miles, and turn left onto Mississippi River Blvd. S. In 0.4 mile turn left onto the ramp for MN 5 W. In 2 miles, take the Post Road exit. Turn left onto Post Road; parking will be on the right in 0.5 mile.

Additional parking can be found along S. Minnehaha Drive south of the John H. Stevens House, along S. Minnehaha Drive farther south near where it intersects Minnehaha Ave., along Hiawatha Ave. near where it intersects with E. 54th St., and just off Godfrey Pkwy./W. River Pkwy. at the entrance to Lock and Dam No. 1.

The Wabun Picnic Area at Minnehaha Regional Park also has ample parking and facilities. Take I-94 to Exit 237. Head south on Cretin Ave. N., and go 2.6 miles. Turn right onto Ford Pkwy., and in 0.8 mile turn left onto 46th Ave. S. In 0.2 mile turn left into the picnic area.

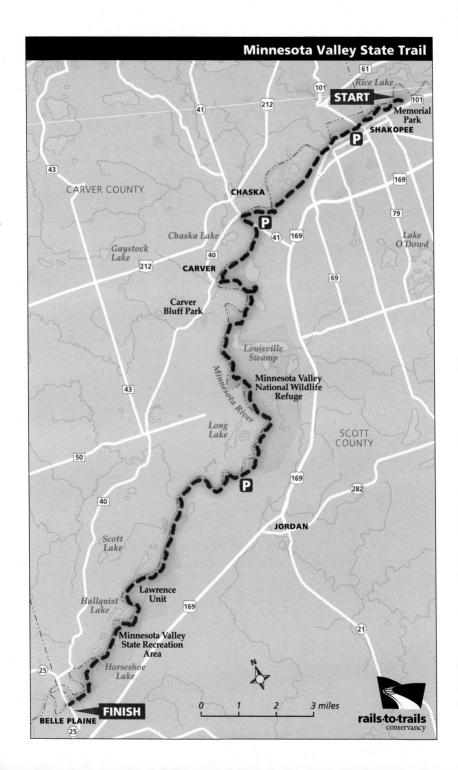

As of spring 2016, bridge access to the Minnesota Valley State Trail was still closed at Memorial Park in Shakopee until further notice. Check the Minnesota Department of Natural Resources website for updates.

The Minnesota Valley State Trail is used by cyclists, equestrians, hikers, snowmobilers, and cross-country skiers. The trail passes through the Minnesota Valley State Recreation Area at its southern end as well as other natural areas along its route. Portions of the trail run parallel to the Minnesota River, which means that it is subject to flooding in high-water years. Along the trail, you'll encounter oak hardwood forests, oak savanna remnants, and hillsides and bluffs featuring scenic overlooks of the Minnesota River below. Wetlands include floodplain marshes, wet meadows, fens, and lakes. Wildlife and wildflowers abound.

Mountain bikers enjoy this route's fun hills and natural surfaces, but the path can be rough in some places.

Location
Scott

Endpoints
Shenandoah Drive and County Road 101 at Memorial Park (Shakopee) to MN 25/N. Walnut St. at the Minnesota River (Belle Plaine)

Mileage
27.1

Type
Rail-Trail

Roughness Index
1–2

Surface
Asphalt, Crushed Stone

Currently, the trail is more than 27 miles long; the 17.6-mile portion of the trail between Belle Plaine and Chaska has a natural surface and can be rough in places. Between MN 41 in Chaska and Stagecoach Road (at the intersection of US 169 and County Road 101) in Shakopee, the 9.5-mile segment of the trail is paved. There are plans to extend the trail to cover a total of 80 miles between Fort Snelling (where work is already under way) and beyond Belle Plaine to Le Sueur.

A portion of the trail traverses the Minnesota Valley State Recreation Area, providing access to trails and natural amenities in the Lawrence and Louisville Swamp Units for a more intimate opportunity to experience the flora and fauna within the floodplain of the Minnesota River. The historic features of the Jabs Farm site and Little Rapids campsite along the Mazomani Trail within the Louisville Swamp section can be accessed off of the Minnesota Valley State Trail.

There are restrooms at the Lawrence Unit as well as in cities and parks along the route.

CONTACT: dnr.state.mn.us/state_trails/minnesota_valley

DIRECTIONS

For parking in Shakopee, take I-494 to Exit 10A for US 169 S. Merge onto US 169, and go 4.7 miles south. Take the exit for Hennepin County 101/Shakopee. Merge onto County Road 101, heading northwest, and go 5.5 miles. Turn right onto Fillmore St., and park at Huber Park.

For parking near Chaska, take I-494 to Exit 11C. Merge onto US 212, and go 9.1 miles west. Take the MN 41/Chestnut St. exit. Turn left onto MN 41/Chestnut St., and go 2.7 miles. Turn right onto the dirt road just past the TRAIL ACCESS sign.

For Lawrence Unit (Minnesota Valley State Recreation Area), take I-494 to Exit 11C. Merge onto US 212, and go 12.7 miles west. Take the CR 11/Jonathan Carver Pkwy. exit. Turn left onto Jonathan Carver Pkwy., and go 2.6 miles. Turn left to stay on Jonathan Carver Pkwy., and go another 3.8 miles. Parking is on the left immediately after crossing the Minnesota River.

This Mississippi River Regional Trail running through eastern Dakota County is a segment of a larger regional trail system that is itself part of the National Park Service's Mississippi National River and Recreation Area.

The northern portion of the Dakota County segment includes a completed, paved 12.3-mile section starting in South Saint Paul and ending in Inver Grove Heights. The Hastings component starts in Spring Lake Park Reserve and goes into the heart of the river city of Hastings, adding another 6.7 miles to the completed trail. The final 9 miles of this trail is currently being developed and is scheduled for completion in 2017, which will bring the length of the Dakota County section to nearly 28 miles when finished.

Beginning in Simon's Ravine, the northern segment of the paved trail follows along a levee and offers a continuous

River views are plentiful as the trail winds through the National Park Service's Mississippi National River and Recreation Area.

Location
Dakota

Endpoints
Simon's Ravine Trailhead at Kaposia Landing Park off Concord St. N. near Butler Ave. (South Saint Paul) to Courthouse Blvd. and US 52 (Inver Grove Heights); Spring Lake Park Reserve at 127th St. E. near Idell Ave. to Third St. E. and Bailey St. (Hastings)

Mileage
19

Type
Rail-Trail

Roughness Index
1

Surface
Asphalt

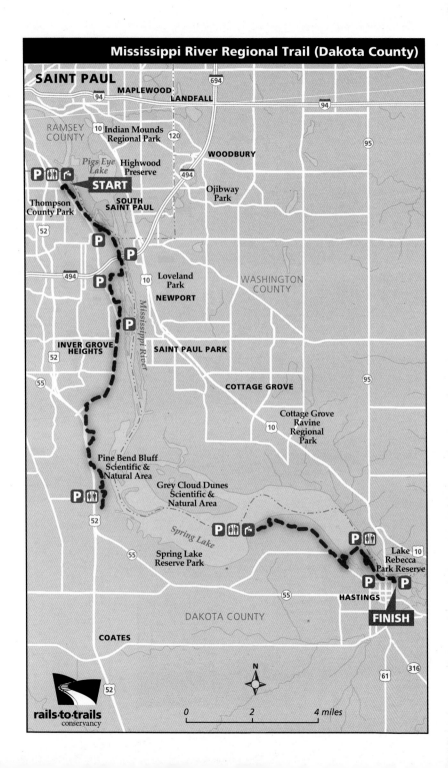

Mississippi River Regional Trail (Dakota County)

overlook view of the railroad and barge commerce on and along the Mississippi River. The middle section of this segment follows city streets through Inver Grove Heights before reaching the lower end of this segment just beyond the wooded, 200-foot bluffs in the Pine Bend Bluff Scientific and Natural Area (one of the least-disturbed natural areas along the Mississippi River in the metro area).

Nine miles of the trail are still under development between Pine Bend Bluff and Schaar's Bluff in Spring Lake Park Reserve, where it picks up again as a 5-mile segment that winds through the bluff-top countryside northwest of Hastings before dropping down and crossing Lock and Dam No. 2 on the Mississippi River. It ends at the southern trailhead terminus in downtown Hastings.

At its northern terminus, the South Saint Paul section of this trail links to another paved trail heading west to Kaposia Park and beyond, called the River to River Greenway. The southern terminus in Hastings connects trail users to a network of trails throughout that city.

Restrooms, parking, and drinking water are available at Kaposia Landing, Simon's Ravine Trailhead, Swing Bridge Trailhead, and Spring Lake Park Reserve.

CONTACT: www.co.dakota.mn.us/parks/parkstrails/mississippiriver

DIRECTIONS

To access Simon's Ravine Trailhead (northern section), from I-94, follow signs for US 10 E. Take Exit 242D to merge onto US 52 S. In 1.9 miles, take the MN 156/Concord St. exit, and turn left onto MN 156 S./Concord St. In 1.9 miles turn left onto Bryant Ave., and parking will be on the right.

To access the south end of the trail, from I-94, follow signs for US 10 E. Take Exit 242D to merge onto US 52 S. In 12.5 miles take the 117th St. exit. Turn left onto 117th St. S.E., and in 0.2 mile turn left onto Courthouse Blvd. The trail is just behind the Pilot Travel Center. There are multiple other access points along the trail.

To access the Hastings trail section (southern section), from I-94, follow signs for US 10 E. Take Exit 242D to merge onto US 52 S. Go 13.6 miles, and take the MN 55 exit. Continue on MN 55/Courthouse Blvd., and go 4.4 miles east. Turn left onto Mississippi Trail, and go 1.7 miles. Turn left onto Idell Ave. In 0.5 mile turn left onto 127th St. E., and go 0.6 mile to reach Schaar's Bluff trailhead in Spring Lake Park Reserve.

To reach the southeastern trailhead in Hastings, take I-94 to Exit 244. Head south on US 10/US 61, and go 18.1 miles, as the road changes to Hastings Road and Vermillion St. Turn left onto Fourth St. E., and in 0.3 mile turn left onto Bailey St. Parking is on the left in one block. Additional parking is available in Lake Rebecca Park Reserve.

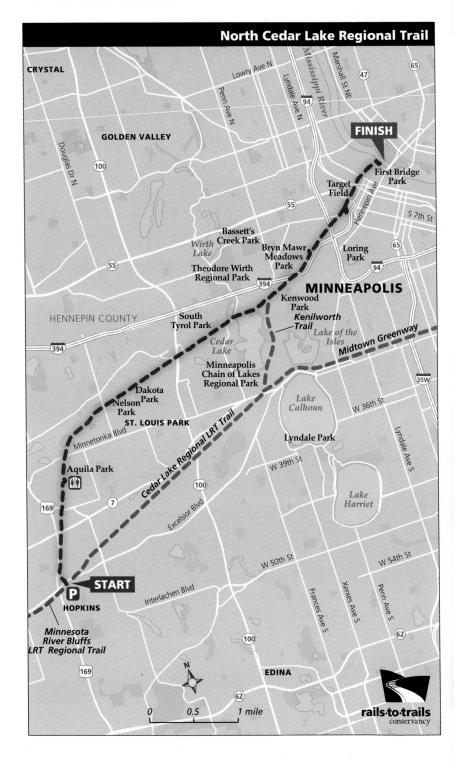

North Cedar Lake Regional Trail

CRYSTAL

Lowry Ave N

Lyndale Ave N

Mississippi River

Marshall St NE

Penn Ave N

47

65

94

GOLDEN VALLEY

Douglas Dr N

100

FINISH

First Bridge Park

Target Field

55

Hennepin Ave

S 7th St

Bassett's Creek Park

Wirth Lake

Bryn Mawr Meadows Park

Loring Park

65

55

Theodore Wirth Regional Park

394

MINNEAPOLIS

94

Kenwood Park

HENNEPIN COUNTY

South Tyrol Park

Kenilworth Trail

Lake of the Isles

Midtown Greenway

394

Cedar Lake

Minneapolis Chain of Lakes Regional Park

35W

Dakota Park

Nelson Park

Lake Calhoun

W 36th St

Lyndale Ave S

ST. LOUIS PARK

Minnetonka Blvd

Lyndale Park

Aquila Park

W 39th St

Lake Harriet

169

7

Cedar Lake Regional LRT Trail

100

Excelsior Blvd

START

W 50th St

W 54th St

HOPKINS

Interlachen Blvd

Frances Ave S

Xerxes Ave S

Penn Ave S

Minnesota River Bluffs LRT Regional Trail

100

62

169

N

EDINA

62

0   0.5   1 mile

rails·to·trails
conservancy

This paved trail links Minneapolis's Warehouse District to both the Minnesota River Bluffs LRT Regional Trail and the Cedar Lake LRT Regional Trail in Hopkins. It also intersects the Kenilworth Trail as part of the Cedar Lake Loop and a trail spur of the Luce Line State Trail coming down south from Theodore Wirth Regional Park along the Bassett Creek Regional Trail.

The trail is mostly urban at the eastern terminus at its junction with the West River Parkway, where the City of Minneapolis segment is most often called the Cedar Lake Trail. As it heads southwest, it passes a more serene landscape through Minneapolis's wooded suburbs. The trail also links many neighborhood parks along the way. From St. Louis Park, where the trail crosses MN 100, to Hopkins, the trail is officially named the North Cedar Lake Regional Trail.

The paved trail traverses a mix of wooded suburbs, neighborhood parks, and urban areas on its way to downtown Minneapolis.

Location
Hennepin

Endpoints
Excelsior Blvd. just east of US 169 (Hopkins) to W. River Pkwy. north of Hennepin Ave. Bridge (Minneapolis)

Mileage
9

Type
Rail-with-Trail

Roughness Index
1

Surface
Asphalt

A part of the trail actually consists of three separate paths: two unidirectional paths for bicyclists and a multidirectional trail for pedestrians. Near the trail's midpoint, bikers and runners will pass the trail's namesake lake. Just east of Cedar Lake, the Kenilworth Trail begins, which takes trail users through the ritzy Kenwood neighborhood to the Cedar Lake LRT Regional Trail. Some consider this to be the nicest part of the trail.

You can also pick up the Luce Line Trail where the North Cedar Lake Regional Trail passes Bryn Mawr Meadows Park to continue on a much longer journey westward. This eastern section of the Luce Line Trail opened in 2002.

In Minneapolis, the trail, often referred to as the bike freeway, runs under Target Field—home to the Minnesota Twins—and immediately next to its rail station. At the trail's terminus in north Minneapolis, connect to the West River Parkway Trail for a pleasant ride or run along the Mississippi River.

CONTACT: threeriversparks.org/trails/north-cedar-lake-trail.aspx

DIRECTIONS

In Hopkins park in the lot at the Depot Coffee House. Take I-394 to Exit 3, and follow US 169 4.2 miles south. Take the Excelsior Blvd./County Road 3 exit. Turn left onto Excelsior Blvd. The coffee house will be on your right in 0.2 mile.

Unofficial parking areas for trail access can be found in Aquila Park on W. 31st St. near Aquila Ave.; just off Virginia Ave. S. at Victoria Lake; St. Louis Park at Nelson and Dakota Parks on W. 26th St. near Dakota Ave.; and at the eastern terminus just south of N. Fourth Ave. near First Bridge Park.

Paul Bunyan State Trail, stretching 123 miles from Bemidji to Brainerd, is one of the longest rail-trails in the country. This distance includes its newest segment, completed in 2014, that extended the trail 9 miles south on MN 371 to Crow Wing State Park. The multiuse, fully paved trail is mainly for nonmotorized use; however, snowmobiles are permitted during winter.

The Paul Bunyan State Trail follows an inactive railroad corridor built in 1893 and last owned by Burlington Northern. The corridor passes through boreal forests, along more than 20 lakes and 10 rivers/streams, and among meadows sporting colorful wildflowers in spring. You'll also encounter wildlife along the way.

For those using the trail for the long haul, you'll find towns situated every 8–10 miles. Many of the towns have a long history in the railroad and timber industries, and, before that, American Indians of the Ojibwe and Dakota

The trail parallels the Mississippi River in Baxter before heading north and west, away from the waterway.

Location
Beltrami, Cass, Crow Wing, Hubbard

Endpoints
County Road 20 and CR 18 at Lake Bemidji State Park (Bemidji) to CR 27 near MN 371 in Crow Wing State Park (Brainerd)

Mileage
123

Type
Rail-Trail

Roughness Index
1

Surface
Asphalt

Paul Bunyan State Trail

Blue Ox Trail

89

BELTRAMI COUNTY

ITASCA COUNTY

SOLWAY   WILTON

2

FINISH

Mississippi Headwaters State Forest

BEMIDJI   Lake Bemidji State Park

71

P

46

Cass Lake

Lake Winnibigoshish

CASS LAKE   **2**

BENA   **2**

Paul Bunyan State Forest

71

Heartland State Trail

Chippewa National Forest

CASS COUNTY

200

200

371

LAPORTE

HUBBARD COUNTY   **64**

BOY RIVER

Leech Lake

71

Paul Bunyan State Forest

WALKER   **P**

REMER

AKELEY

200

84

6

Heartland State Trail

P

LONGVILLE

NEVIS   **34**

HACKENSACK   **P**

PARK RAPIDS

Badoura State Forest   **64**

BACKUS   **87**

87

87

CHICKAMAW BEACH

Huntersville State Forest

Foot Hills State Forest

EMILY

MENAHGA

PINE RIVER

71

JENKINS   **P**

227

64

PEQUOT LAKES   **P**

SEBEKA

NIMROD

WADENA COUNTY

CASS COUNTY

Crow Wing State Forest

Lyons State Forest

NISSWA   **P**

LAKE SHORE

IRONTON

WADENA

Pillsbury State Forest

RIVERTON

P   **210**

VERNDALE

10   ALDRICH

EAST GULL LAKE

HEWITT

210   STAPLES

MOTLEY   Crow Wing River   **210**   BAXTER   **P**   BRAINERD   **18**

71

10

Crow Wing State Park

START   **371**

CROW WING COUNTY

25

Mississippi River

N

0   7   14 miles

FORT RIPLEY

rails·to·trails
conservancy

nations lived in the region. Those wishing to camp during their trip can do so at either end of the trail: at Crow Wing State Park or at Lake Bemidji State Park in Bemidji.

The Paul Bunyan State Trail intersects with the Heartland State Trail at MN 34 northeast of Akeley and north of Walker near MN 200 and MN 371. The Paul Bunyan State Trail also connects with the Blue Ox Trail at Paul Bunyan's northern trailhead in Lake Bemidji State Park, although the actual northern end of the trail (with no parking or amenities) is just northeast of the park at CR 20.

There are five newly installed bicycle repair stations along the trail at the following locations: Northland Arboretum parking lot and trailhead in Brainerd; Lake Bemidji State Park visitor center; Crow Wing State Park, near the trail start; Nisswa; and Pine River.

The Paul Bunyan State Trail between Nisswa and Jenkins will remain open during the MN 371 North realignment project expected to last through fall 2016.

To allow for highway realignment, a new section of trail that will become a permanent reroute is to be constructed in summer 2016. The trail realignment is expected to cause minimal disruptions. As always, trail users should be cautious near construction activity and check trail conditions before traveling.

For construction updates, trail conditions, and more information, visit **dnr .state.mn.us/state_trails/paul_bunyan**.

CONTACT: paulbunyantrail.com

DIRECTIONS

To reach the southern trailhead at Crow Wing State Park, from the intersection of MN 210 and MN 371 in Baxter, take MN 371 S. 7.5 miles to 60th Ave. S.W./N. Koering Road. Follow it northwest 1.3 miles through Crow Wing State Park to the parking lot, which will be on your right.

To reach the parking lot in Baxter, from the intersection of MN 210 and the MN 371 bypass in Baxter, go north one block on MN 371 to Excelsior Road. Turn right onto Excelsior and go 0.75 mile to Conservation Drive; the parking lot is on the left.

The northern trailhead is located in Lake Bemidji State Park. From the intersection of US 71 and US 2/MN 197/Paul Bunyan Drive in Bemidji, head east on Paul Bunyan Drive 1.6 miles. Turn left onto Bemidji Ave. N., and go 3.9 miles. Turn right onto Birchmont Beach Road/County Road 20 and go 1.5 miles to the park's entrance. Follow State Park Road 1 mile to the trailhead.

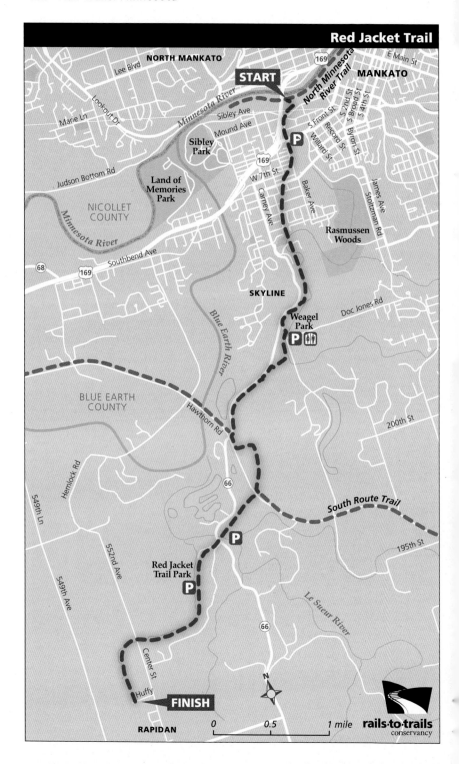

Red Jacket Trail

NORTH MANKATO

MANKATO

START

FINISH

RAPIDAN

SKYLINE

Sibley Park

Land of Memories Park

NICOLLET COUNTY

BLUE EARTH COUNTY

Weagel Park

Rasmussen Woods

Red Jacket Trail Park

North Minnesota River Trail

South Route Trail

Minnesota River

Blue Earth River

Le Sueur River

Lee Blvd

Lookout Dr

Marie Ln

Judson Bottom Rd

Southbend Ave

Sibley Ave

Mound Ave

W. 7th St

Carney Ave

Baker Ave

Hawthorn Rd

Hemlock Rd

549th Ln

552nd Ave

549th Ave

Center St

Huffy

Doc Jones Rd

200th St

195th St

James Ave

Stoltzman Rd

S Front St

Record St

Willard St

S 2nd St

S Broad St

Byron St

S 4th St

E Main St

169

169

68

169

66

66

0   0.5   1 mile

rails·to·trails
conservancy

Named after a Seneca Indian chief who lived in the area until the 1830s, the Red Jacket Trail runs along an old Milwaukee Road (formerly the Minnesota Railroad and the Central Railroad) right-of-way that became inactive in 1978. The Red Jacket Trail begins at the restored depot along the banks of the Minnesota River, west of downtown Mankato, and runs to the village of Rapidan. In Mankato, the trail branches off from the North Minnesota River Trail, which continues along the waterway to the Sakatah Singing Hills State Trail.

The popular Red Jacket Trail utilizes three converted railroad trestles, including the stunning Red Jacket Trestle, which is more than 80 feet high and 550 feet long and traverses the Le Sueur River and busy MN 66 near the trail's southern end. Major floods in 2010 damaged one of the trestle's abutments, forcing the bridge to close. The trestle

Heavily wooded forest shades most of the route.

Location
Blue Earth

Endpoints
North Minnesota River Trail under US 169 near Poplar St. (Mankato) to Huffy Lane just west of 552nd Ave. (Rapidan)

Mileage
13

Type
Rail-Trail

Roughness Index
1–2

Surface
Asphalt, Crushed Stone

has since been repaired and is back in full service. Two smaller bridges cross just a mile or two south of the Red Jacket Trestle.

The Red Jacket Trail extends southward away from downtown Mankato, passing commercial properties before cutting directly through one of the city's older neighborhoods. After about 1 mile, the scenery changes to heavily wooded forest; this landscape continues for the rest of the trek to Rapidan.

At Hawthorn Road, a short section of trail is shared with the South Route Trail, which takes bikers and walkers northwest along County Road 90 for about 4 miles to the southern section of Minneopa State Park. A pure strain of American bison was introduced to the park's northern section in the fall of 2015.

Before reaching Rapidan, be sure to spend time at Red Jacket Trail Park. The park contains a picnic shelter, canoe launch, and parking lot, and offers breathtaking views of the trestle. In Rapidan, follow the paved shoulder on 552nd Avenue a short distance south to access the heart of the small village.

A noteworthy side trip is to follow CR 9 west from Rapidan about 2 miles to Rapidan Dam Park for more parking, restrooms, and an expansive view of the Blue Earth River Valley.

CONTACT: blueearthcountymn.gov/facilities/facility/details /red-jacket-trail-park-7

DIRECTIONS

In Mankato, parking can be found downtown, about one block east of US 169 where it intersects with S. Riverfront Drive. Take I-35 to Exit 56. Turn left (southwest) onto MN 60, and go 31.1 miles. Turn right onto US 14, and go 8 miles. Take the Riverfront Drive exit, and turn left onto Riverfront Drive. Go 2.7 miles, and turn right onto Stoltzman Road, where parking is available. The trail is one block west.

Mankato Area Public Schools and Mankato Family YMCA both have large parking lots adjacent to the trail.

Just southwest of Mankato, parking and portable toilets are located at Weagel Park. Take I-35 to Exit 56. Turn left (southwest) onto MN 60, and go 31.1 miles. Turn right onto US 14, and go 10.1 miles. Take the MN 60/US 169 exit toward Mankato. In 2.9 miles take the Riverfront Drive exit toward MN 66. Turn right onto S. Riverfront Drive, and in 0.2 mile turn left onto Sibley St. In 0.2 mile turn right onto W. Seventh St. Take the first left onto MN 66/Carney Ave. In 1.4 miles turn left onto Indian Lake Road, and parking will be on the right.

Additional parking and a picnic shelter are located at Red Jacket Trail Park. Take I-35 to Exit 56. Turn left (southwest) onto MN 60, and go 31.1 miles. Turn right onto US 14, and go 6 miles. Take the MN 22 exit, and turn left onto MN 22. Go 4.8 miles, and turn right onto County Road 90. Turn left onto MN 66, and go 0.7 mile. Turn left, and parking will be on the right.

Minnesota's Rocori Trail, named for the three small towns through which it will eventually run (Rockville, Cold Spring, and Richmond), currently has two disconnected segments open for use.

The first section of trail opened in 2009 in the quaint downtown area of Rockville. Built during the reconstruction of Broadway Street/County Road 82, the 1-mile stretch of trail is immediately adjacent to the road, allowing for easy access to residences, businesses, and city hall.

A newer, longer portion of trail opened in 2012 between 178th Avenue, roughly halfway between Cold Spring and Richmond, and the eastern city limit of Cold Spring at the Sauk River. This 3-mile section uses a former BNSF Railway corridor and is parallel to MN 23 for nearly

A highlight of the trail is the bridge over the Sauk River in Cold Spring.

Location
Stearns

Endpoints
178th Ave. and MN 23 to Sauk River Road and Second Ave. N.E. (Cold Spring); Chestnut St. to Pine St. along Broadway St. (Rockville)

Mileage
3.1

Type
Rail-Trail

Roughness Index
1

Surface
Asphalt

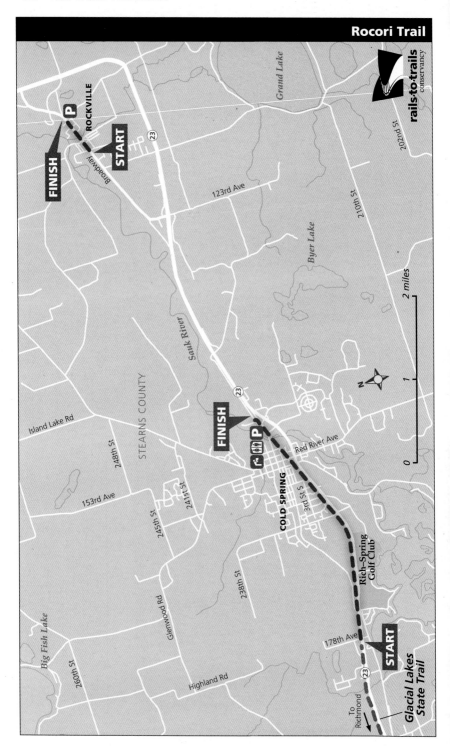

Rocori Trail

its entire length. At 178th Avenue the trail seamlessly connects to the Glacial Lakes State Trail.

The headquarters of Coldspring (formerly the Cold Spring Granite company), nationally known for contributing to both the FDR Memorial and Korean War Veterans Memorial in Washington, D.C., is located at the trail's western terminus. Other sites along the way include the Cold Spring Baseball Park (a short trek up Seventh Avenue in Cold Spring) and the sprawling Rich-Spring Golf Club (across MN 23 from the trail).

Features along this short trail include views of the Sauk River, the Rockville granite quarry, Cold Spring dam and waterfall, and scenic countryside and parks.

Funding is being sought to develop the trail linking the existing segments in Cold Spring and Rockville together by 2017 or sooner. The project will include the rehabilitation of an original railroad trestle over the Sauk River. Longer-term plans also call for extending this trail east all the way to St. Cloud. Besides the Glacial Lakes State Trail, the Rocori Trail is part of a network of trails, including the Lake Wobegon Trail and the Lake Koronis Recreational Trail in Paynesville.

CONTACT: tinyurl.com/rocori

DIRECTIONS

To reach the segment in Rockville, take I-94 to Exit 164. Head southwest on MN 23, and go 3.2 miles. Turn right onto County Road 82/Broadway St. You can park and access the trail anywhere along Broadway St.

To reach the trailhead on the Sauk River in Cold Spring, take I-94 to Exit 164. Head southwest on MN 23, and go 9 miles. Turn right onto Main St.; parking is located on the right in 0.2 mile.

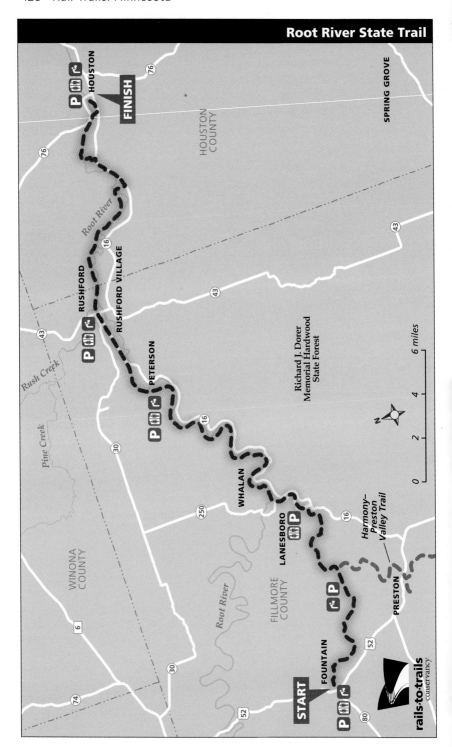

Root River State Trail

START

FINISH

HOUSTON

RUSHFORD

RUSHFORD VILLAGE

PETERSON

WHALAN

LANESBORO

FOUNTAIN

PRESTON

SPRING GROVE

HOUSTON COUNTY

WINONA COUNTY

FILLMORE COUNTY

Root River

Rush Creek

Pine Creek

Root River

Richard J. Dorer Memorial Hardwood State Forest

Harmony–Preston Valley Trail

rails-to-trails conservancy

6 miles

0   2   4

N

76

76

43

43

43

16

16

16

16

30

30

30

250

6

74

52

52

80

Along much of its route, the Root River State Trail follows the winding course of its namesake river for 42 miles through the Minnesota towns of Fountain, Lanesboro, Whalan, Peterson, Rushford, and Houston. The paved trail is mostly level, although a section just west of Houston (around Money Creek Woods) has some steep hills for about 0.5 mile.

Along the way, you'll have outstanding views of the tall limestone bluffs and the steep hills thickly wooded in maples and birch that rise above the river. Watch for wildlife, such as turkeys, deer, raccoons, and birds of prey. You might also encounter rattlesnakes sunning themselves on rock outcrops or along the river bottom and trail. Rattlesnakes are a protected state species and should be left alone.

The towns along the route provide many amenities, including bed-and-breakfasts, campgrounds, restaurants, museums, outfitters, and interesting shops and historical

The trail crosses the lushly wooded Root River several times.

Location
Fillmore, Houston

Endpoints
County Road 8 at Maple St. (Fountain) to W. Plum St. near MN 76/N. Grant St. (Houston)

Mileage
42

Type
Rail-Trail

Roughness Index
1

Surface
Asphalt

buildings. The trail is built on an old railroad right-of-way that followed the river, linking rural communities throughout this alluring tourism region of southeastern Minnesota.

Cross-country skiing is popular during winter, and the trail intersects with a system of groomed snowmobile trails. Between Lanesboro and Fountain, the trail meets up with the 18-mile-long Harmony–Preston Valley State Trail. There is an access point on the Root River State Trail at Isinours Management Unit, with parking available about 0.5 mile west of the northern trailhead for the Harmony–Preston Valley State Trail, just beyond County Road 17. The combined Root River/Harmony–Preston Valley network provides more than 60 miles of paved trails through Minnesota's most scenic bluff country.

Every trailhead in the towns along the route has a bicycle tune-up station. Restrooms are at every official trailhead along the route, except in Whalan.

CONTACT: rootrivertrail.org

DIRECTIONS

To reach parking in Fountain, take I-90 to Exit 218. Turn left (south) onto US 52, and go 21.3 miles. Turn left onto County Road 8, and in 0.3 mile reach the parking lot near the city park/softball field on the right.

In Lanesboro parking is available on the street and at the lot by the Lanesboro Community Center and Sylvan Park. Take I-90 to Exit 218. Turn left (south) onto US 52, and go 21.3 miles. Turn left onto CR 8, and in 9.1 miles turn right onto Parkway Ave. S. In 0.2 mile Sylvan Park is on the left. Trail access is 0.2 mile north at CR 8/Elmwood St.

Parking is available near the midpoint in Peterson. Take I-90 to Exit 242. Head south on CR 29, and go 1.6 miles. Turn left to stay on CR 29, and go 5.6 miles. Continue straight on CR 25, which becomes S. Church St., and go 5.8 miles. Turn right onto Park St., and immediately turn right onto Fillmore St. to reach the city park. The bike station is located on the trail at the intersection of Park St. and S. Church St./CR 25.

For the eastern trailhead, take I-90 to Exit 258. Head south on MN 76, and go 13.5 miles. Turn right onto W. Plum St. Parking will be on the right.

This trail is so nice they named it twice: *Sakatah* is the Dakota word for "singing hills." The Dakota people of the Great Sioux Nation originally lived in this scenic part of Minnesota, where the Big Woods once met the prairie. A rail line was built through the area in the late 19th century and rendered inactive by Chicago and North Western in the 1970s. In 1980 the Minnesota Department of Natural Resources opened the route, which it had acquired as a rail-trail shortly after it went inactive.

The Sakatah Singing Hills State Trail runs through a beautiful landscape of farmland, lakes, wetlands, and woods. The two anchor towns of Faribault (on the eastern end) and Mankato (to the west) are the trail's largest and are home to many restaurants and shops. In Waterville, near the trail's midpoint, the trail leaves the former railroad corridor for a short signed detour on city streets. Other towns on the route are smaller, but can serve as refreshing rest stops.

Although the trail is paved for its entire length, conditions vary. Rough trail segments exist along the 13.5-mile

The trail offers diverse scenery, from Minnesota hardwoods to open prairie.

Location
Blue Earth, Le Sueur, Rice

Endpoints
N. Riverfront Drive and US 14 (Mankato) to MN 21 north of Seventh St. N.W. (Faribault)

Mileage
39

Type
Rail-Trail

Roughness Index
1

Surface
Asphalt

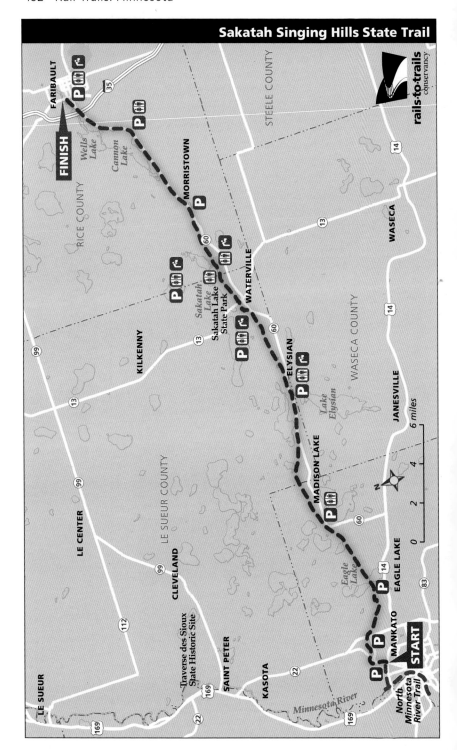

Sakatah Singing Hills State Trail

section between Madison Lake and Waterville. In 2012 a 10.5-mile section from Morristown to Faribault was repaved. In the fall of 2015, a section of the trail between County Road 12 and Madison Lake was closed for construction, and the process of milling and repaving this segment began.

At times, the trail runs immediately adjacent to several large lakes, including Wells Lake, Cannon Lake, Sakatah Lake, Lake Elysian, and Eagle Lake. Be sure to stop for an extended rest at Sakatah Lake State Park; the trail runs through the park for 3 miles and the area is a great place to picnic, hike, or swim. In Mankato connect directly with the North Minnesota River Trail, which leads to the Red Jacket Trail and its stunning trestle over the Blue Earth River. In Faribault, the planned Mill Towns Trail will eventually link the Sakatah Singing Hills State Trail with the existing Cannon Valley Trail. The addition of that proposed 20-mile segment from Mankato to Red Wing (the eastern endpoint of the Cannon Valley Trail) would create a trail just shy of 100 miles long on a single converted railroad corridor.

CONTACT: dnr.state.mn.us/state_trails/sakatah

DIRECTIONS

The primary western trailhead is located in Mankato at a small parking lot on Lime Valley Road, just north of US 14. The actual trail end is south of US 14 at W. Dukes St. Take I-35 to Exit 56. Turn left (southwest) onto MN 60, and go 31.1 miles. Turn right onto US 14, and go 8 miles to the Riverfront Drive exit. Turn right onto N. Riverfront Drive, and in 0.6 mile turn left onto Lime Valley Road. Parking will be on the left in 0.25 mile.

In Faribault, park at White Sands Park. Take I-35 to Exit 59. Turn right (southeast) onto MN 21/Lyndale Ave., and go 1.6 miles. White Sands Park is on the right.

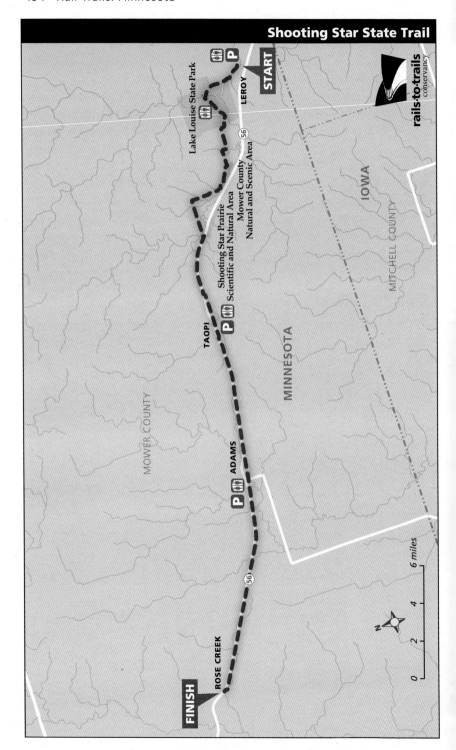

Shooting Star State Trail

rails·to·trails
conservancy

START

LEROY

Lake Louise State Park

56

Mower County
Natural and Scenic Area

Shooting Star Prairie
Scientific and Natural Area

TAOPI

MINNESOTA

IOWA

MITCHELL COUNTY

MOWER COUNTY

ADAMS

56

ROSE CREEK

FINISH

N

0   2   4   6 miles

Shooting Star State Trail, currently 19 miles long, is an 8-foot-wide asphalt path from LeRoy (east) to Rose Creek (west). It follows an unused railroad bed on Milwaukee Road, which once stretched from the Midwest through the Rocky Mountains.

The eastern end of the trail begins in LeRoy, just 0.25 mile beyond Lake Louise State Park. The trail winds through open meadows and hardwood groves before emerging onto the agricultural fields to the west. The trail then skirts both the Mower County Natural and Scenic Area and the Shooting Star Prairie Scientific and Natural Area as it heads west through the communities of Taopi and Adams and, finally, to the western trailhead at Rose Creek.

The Shooting Star State Trail is named after the colorful native shooting star wildflower.

Location
Mower

Endpoints
W. Lowell St. near 770th Ave. (LeRoy) to 170th St. at MN 56 (Rose Creek)

Mileage
18.8

Type
Rail-Trail

Roughness Index
1

Surface
Asphalt

Midway between Adams and Rose Creek, a memorial in the form of a Norwegian church has been erected as a rest stop in honor of Margie Meier, a staunch supporter of the trail. The scenic trail includes bike racks and rest benches in key places along the route.

Construction has begun on an 8-mile western extension of the trail from Rose Creek to Austin and is expected to be completed by the summer of 2016.

Restrooms and picnic areas are available in LeRoy, Lake Louise State Park, Taopi, and the Adam City Park and Campground on the west side of town.

CONTACT: shootingstartrail.org

DIRECTIONS

To reach the LeRoy trailhead, from I-90, take Exit 209A. Turn left onto MN 30/US 63, and go 12.3 miles south. Turn right onto MN 16, and go 1.5 miles. Turn left onto 770th Ave., and go 13.6 miles. Turn left onto W. Lowell St. Ample parking is available at the trailhead between 770th Ave. and N. Mather St.

Parking is also available in Adams north of Main St. in Adams City Park. Take I-90 to Exit 193. Head east on MN 16, and in 0.3 mile turn right onto County Road 7/670th Ave. In 9.3 miles veer left onto 665th Ave., and go 1.5 miles. Turn right onto W. Main St., and in 0.3 mile turn left onto Adams Park Road.

Ample parking is also available at the Rose Creek trailhead. Take I-90 to Exit 187. Head north on MN 20, and immediately turn left onto 220th St. In 1.8 miles turn left onto 610th Ave. In 5.5 miles turn left onto 170th St./Maple St. S.E. Parking will be on the right.

The St. Anthony Falls Heritage Trail is a 1.8-mile loop along the Minneapolis riverfront within the St. Anthony Falls National Register Historic District. Maps, finding aids, and the area's geological, engineering, and industrial history are related on trail markers. Signs include the stories of American Indians, early white settlers, and individuals and groups related to the falls.

The signature feature of this trail is the Stone Arch Bridge, which is the only one of its kind over the Mississippi River. Built in 1883 by the Great Northern Railway tycoon James J. Hill, it facilitated the movement of people and goods across the river by rail until 1978. Consisting of 23 arches made from native granite and limestone, the 28-foot side bridge stretches for 2,100 feet, spanning the Mississippi River below St. Anthony Falls.

The bridge provided a link between the midway section of Saint Paul and the East Bank Mills in Minneapolis. It was also part of the region's early railroad network, which made each train line responsible for finding its own route into Union Depot in downtown Minneapolis.

As it crosses the Mississippi River, the path offers a fantastic vista of the downtown Minneapolis skyline.

Location
Hennepin

Endpoints
Sixth Ave. S.E. and S.E. Main St. in Father Hennepin Bluff Park to W. River Pkwy. and Hennepin Ave. (Minneapolis)

Mileage
1.8

Type
Rail-Trail

Roughness Index
1

Surface
Asphalt

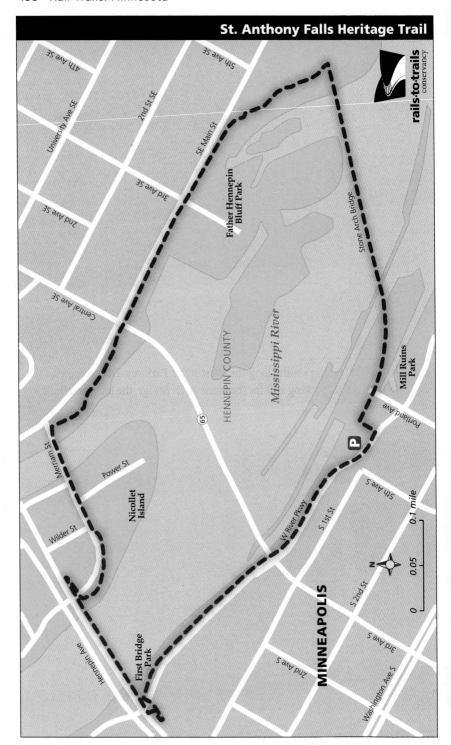

St. Anthony Falls Heritage Trail

rails-to-trails
conservancy

4th Ave SE

University Ave SE

2nd St SE

5th Ave SE

SE Main St

3rd Ave SE

2nd Ave SE

Central Ave SE

Father Hennepin
Bluff Park

Stone Arch Bridge

Mill Ruins
Park

HENNEPIN COUNTY

Mississippi River

Portland Ave

65

Merriam St

Power St

Nicollet
Island

Wilder St

W River Pkwy

S 1st St

5th Ave S

P

First Bridge
Park

Hennepin Ave

MINNEAPOLIS

S 2nd St.

2nd Ave S

3rd Ave S

Washington Ave S

N

0   0.05   0.1 mile

Designated as a national Historical Civil Engineering Landmark, the Stone Arch Bridge sat idle for more than a decade beginning in the 1980s. A group of private and public organizations began refurbishing the landmark, which reopened as a pedestrian/bike bridge in 1994.

The short riverfront loop takes trail users across the bridge, providing a spectacular vantage point to view St. Anthony Falls immediately upriver from the span or downriver toward the University of Minnesota campus and the Dinkytown Greenway bridge, the next walk/bike bridge that crosses the river a short way downstream.

The trail passes next to Father Hennepin Bluff Park before following along Southeast Main Street, a riverfront section of retail shops and eateries. There is an option at Father Hennepin Bluff Park to head along streets toward the main university campus to the southeast, where trail users can link up with the Dinkytown Greenway trail that crosses the river about 0.75 mile to the southeast.

Otherwise, beyond these storefronts, the Heritage Trail crosses Nicollet Island, passing a pavilion on Merriam Street, before crossing the Hennepin Avenue Bridge back toward downtown Minneapolis.

Immediately down off the Hennepin Avenue Bridge, the trail passes through First Bridge Park on the West River Parkway for an opportunity to continue north, south (Minnehaha Falls is 6 miles away), and west to other major Minneapolis trail networks. Heading south along the West River Parkway Trail completes the loop at the trailhead/parking area for the Stone Arch Bridge, the lock, and the dam as well as other historic landmarks in this old mill district complex along the river.

CONTACT: mnhs.org/places/safhb/things_heritage.php

DIRECTIONS

From I-35W N. take Exit 18, and turn right onto University Ave. S.E. In 0.1 mile turn right onto 11th Ave. S.E., which becomes Second St. S.E. In 0.4 mile turn left onto Sixth Ave. S.E., and enter Father Hennepin Bluff Park. From I-35W S., take Exit 18, and turn right onto S.E. Fourth St. In 0.3 mile turn left onto Fifth Ave. S.E., and go 0.2 mile to the park.

From I-35W S., take Exit 17C. Turn right onto S. Washington Ave., and in 0.5 mile turn right onto Portland Ave. In 0.1 mile turn left onto W. River Pkwy. The Stone Arch Bridge parking area is on the right. From I-35W N., take Exit 16A, and keep left, following signs for downtown. Continue on MN 65 1 mile. Continue on Fifth Ave. S. 0.6 mile, and turn right onto S. Washington Ave. Immediately turn left onto Portland Ave. S., and in 0.1 mile turn left onto W. River Pkwy. The Stone Arch Bridge parking area is on the right.

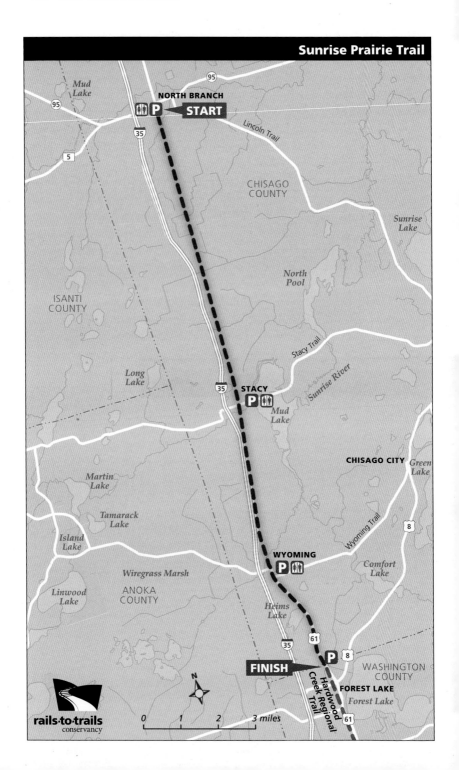

Sunrise Prairie Trail

45 Sunrise Prairie Trail

The Sunrise Prairie Trail runs north-south atop an unused right-of-way along a Burlington Northern Railroad corridor, traversing residential neighborhoods in the towns and mostly farmland in its middle section. The trail also runs through hardwood forests and crosses several wetland areas. It crosses both the west and the south branch of the Sunrise River before changing to the Hardwood Creek Regional Trail in downtown Forest Lake. Wildlife is abundant, and you may see grouse, white-tailed deer, wild turkey, and waterfowl, in addition to native prairie and wildflowers.

The trailhead in North Branch, located at the intersection of MN 95 and Forest Boulevard/County Road 30, offers ample parking, restrooms, and a picnic area. More facilities are available at the midway trail access in Stacy, including parking, restrooms, and water. One mile south

The fully paved, level trail provides an easy way for families to enjoy outdoor recreation in eastern Minnesota.

Location
Chisago

Endpoints
Maple St. and Forest Blvd. (North Branch) to US 61 and 240th St. N. (Forest Lake)

Mileage
16.2

Type
Rail-Trail

Roughness Index
1

Surface
Asphalt

of the trail's crossing of the South Branch of the Sunrise River, the town of Wyoming has a toilet.

The trail becomes the Hardwood Creek Regional Trail once it reaches West Broadway Avenue in downtown Forest Lake. Combined, the two trails provide more than 24 miles of trails between North Branch and Hugo. Although snowmobiles are technically prohibited, you will still find them along the trail during winter. The uncrowded, low-trafficked stretches between towns make the Sunrise Prairie Trail an excellent route for uninterrupted training rides.

CONTACT: co.chisago.mn.us/480/sunrise-prairie-trail

DIRECTIONS

In North Branch, take I-35 to Exit 147. Go 0.6 mile east on MN 95 to Forest Blvd./County Road 30. Turn right, go south one block, and turn right onto Maple St. to reach the trailhead on the southwest corner of the intersection of Forest Blvd. and Maple St.

The Stacy trailhead is located just off the I-35 exit. Take I-35 to Exit 139. Head 0.3 mile east on Stacy Trail/CR 19 to Lions Park on the right.

In Wyoming take I-35 to Exit 135 for US 61/Chisago County Road 22. Head 0.2 mile east on US 61/E. Viking Blvd. Turn left onto Forest Blvd., and go approximately 300 feet to the trailhead on the left. Public restrooms are available in the Giese Memorial Library across from the parking lot.

In Forest Lake, park at US 61 and Broadway Ave. Take I-35 to Exit 131. Head east 0.8 mile on W. Broadway Ave. Parking is on the left just after crossing US 61.

Developed in 1988, the Western Waterfront Trail (WWT) offers direct access to the shoreline of the St. Louis River estuary in southwestern Duluth. The trail begins right across the street from the northern trailhead of the Willard Munger State Trail. The WWT is a 10-foot-wide, tree-lined gravel corridor through commercial, residential, and natural areas as it follows the 9-mile shoreline of the St. Louis River estuary.

The trail skirts the edges of residential neighborhoods but is mainly a nature corridor that passes through marsh environments with opportunities to observe more than 270 species of birds and aquatic mammals along with views of the St. Louis River where it empties into Lake Superior.

In spring 2015, the city of Duluth began the Western Waterfront Restoration, Renewal and Access project,

The route offers beautiful, natural surroundings near the shoreline of the St. Louis River.

Location
St. Louis

Endpoints
Pulaski St. and Bayhill Drive, east to S. 63rd Ave. W. north of Fremont St., and west to Spring St. and W. Penton Blvd. (Duluth)

Mileage
3.2

Type
Rail-Trail (short section)

Roughness Index
2

Surface
Crushed Gravel

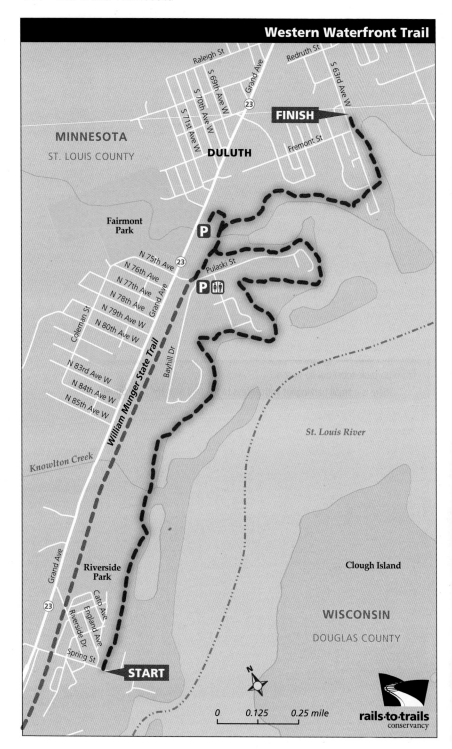

Western Waterfront Trail

Raleigh St

Redruth St

S 69th Ave W

Grand Ave

S 70th Ave W

S 71st Ave W

S 63rd Ave W

23

FINISH

MINNESOTA

ST. LOUIS COUNTY

DULUTH

Fremont St

Fairmont
Park

P

N 75th Ave

23

Pulaski St

P

N 76th Ave

N 77th Ave

N 78th Ave

N 79th Ave W

N 80th Ave W

Grand Ave

Coleman St

N 83rd Ave W

N 84th Ave W

N 85th Ave W

William Munger State Trail

Bayhill Dr

St. Louis River

Knowlton Creek

Clough Island

Grand Ave

23

Riverside
Park

Cato Ave

England Ave

Riverside Dr

Spring St

WISCONSIN

DOUGLAS COUNTY

START

N

0   0.125   0.25 mile

rails·to·trails
conservancy

which widened the trail and will replace and regrade the gravel trail, and resurface boardwalks and bridges. Universal access upgrades along the trail are also planned. Development goals include extending the trail west from the Riverside area to Morgan Park. These trail improvements are scheduled for completion by December 2016.

Hikers in the Duluth area are close to several of Minnesota's premier northern-route trail systems, including the Willard Munger State Trail that heads south through Jay Cooke State Park and the rugged Superior Hiking Trail and the Gitchi-Gami State Trail that continue the trail system to the north along the shore and ridgeline of Lake Superior. The Western Waterfront Trail shares the Minnesota north-country personality of these trails as being one of the best viewing sites for wildlife habitat in the Duluth area.

CONTACT: **duluthtrails.com/western-waterfront**

DIRECTIONS

In southwest Duluth, take I-35 N. to Exit 251A. Merge onto Cody St., and in 0.2 mile turn right onto N. 63rd Ave. W. In 0.6 mile take a slight right onto MN 23/Grand Ave., and go 1 mile. Turn left onto Pulaski St., and go east one block to the trailhead parking lot on the left (here you'll find a portable toilet but no water).

There is a small parking lot with access to the trail near the Lake Superior Zoo, located just south of the intersection of Grand Ave. and S. 72nd Ave. W. To reach it, follow the directions above, but only go 0.8 mile on MN 23/Grand Ave. The lot is on the left.

Access is also available from neighborhood streets at Spring St. and at S. 63rd Ave. W.

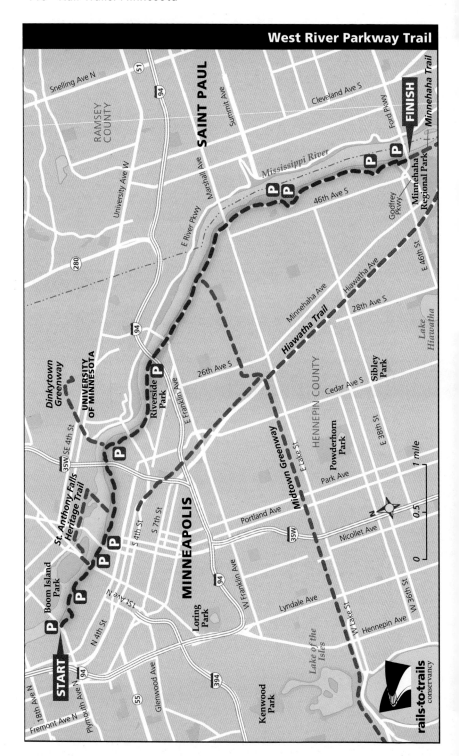

West River Parkway Trail

Snelling Ave N

SAINT PAUL

Cleveland Ave S

Ford Pkwy

FINISH

RAMSEY COUNTY

University Ave W

Summit Ave

Marshall Ave

Mississippi River

46th Ave S

Godfrey Pkwy

Minnehaha Trail

Minnehaha Regional Park

E River Pkwy

E 46th St

Minnehaha Ave

Hiawatha Ave

28th Ave S

Hiawatha Trail

Lake Hiawatha

Dinkytown Greenway

UNIVERSITY OF MINNESOTA

Riverside Park

26th Ave S

E Franklin Ave

HENNEPIN COUNTY

Cedar Ave S

Sibley Park

E 38th St

E 36th St

35W   SE 4th St

St. Anthony Falls Heritage Trail

Midtown Greenway

Powderhorn Park

Park Ave

1 mile

S 7th St

S 4th St

MINNEAPOLIS

Portland Ave

35W

Nicollet Ave

0.5

Boom Island Park

N 4th St

1st Ave N

W Franklin Ave

Lyndale Ave

W Lake St

E Lake St

W 36th St

Hennepin Ave

N

0

START

18th Ave N

Fremont Ave N

Plymouth Ave N

94

Glenwood Ave

55

Loring Park

394

Kenwood Park

Lake of the Isles

rails-to-trails conservancy

51

94

280

94

The West River Parkway Trail, also known as the Mississippi River Gorge Regional Trail, extends between Plymouth Avenue North opposite Boom Island and Ford Parkway in Minnehaha Regional Park, where you can join the Minnehaha Trail.

The trail follows the Mississippi River south (downstream) from north of Plymouth Avenue to Minnehaha Falls and offers spectacular views of the river as well as access to downtown Minneapolis, the University of Minnesota campus, and several trailhead/access points to other urban trails, including the St. Anthony Falls Heritage Trail, the Dinkytown Greenway, and the Midtown Greenway.

The West River Parkway Trail mixes urban amenities with natural areas and is well used for recreation and

As it winds along the Mississippi River, the path delivers spectacular views of the waterway and the Minneapolis skyline.

Location
Hennepin

Endpoints
Plymouth Ave. and W. River Pkwy. opposite Boom Island to Ford Pkwy. and Godfrey Pkwy. at Minnehaha Regional Park (Minneapolis)

Mileage
8.9

Type
Rail-Trail

Roughness Index
1

Surface
Asphalt, Concrete

commuting. The James I. Rice Park at Plymouth Avenue is the first of several parks along the route, most of which have portable toilets, water, and picnic areas, all in settings that offer views of the Mississippi River. The trail runs amid a tree-lined boulevard all along the southern portion of the parkway and offers occasional glimpses of the river far below.

An example of an oak savanna community of plants is being restored along the route at East 36th Street. The 5-mile round-trip Winchell Trail winds along the slopes below the parkway between Franklin Avenue and 44th Street.

A portion of the trail just north of the Franklin Avenue Bridge has been closed for more than a year because of construction to repair damage from a landslide that flushed 4,000 cubic yards of earth off the embankment along the parkway.

The West River Parkway Trail is part of the Grand Rounds National Scenic Byway, a 50-mile loop tour of the region that can be walked, biked, or driven and which features cultural and natural sites. The West River Parkway links up to the Godfrey Parkway, connecting it to Minnehaha Falls and several trails heading farther south.

CONTACT: metrobiketrails.weebly.com/hennepin-county.html#westriver

DIRECTIONS

To reach the northern trailhead from I-94 E., take Exit 229. Turn left onto W. Broadway Ave., and in 0.3 mile turn right onto W. River Road. In 0.5 mile parking will be on the left. From I-94 W., take Exit 229. Continue straight on 17th Ave. N., and in 0.2 mile turn right onto W. River Road. In 0.3 mile parking will be on the left.

There are several parking lots along W. River Pkwy.

To reach the southern trailhead from I-94 just north of downtown Minneapolis, take Exit 237. Head south on Cretin Ave. N., and go 2.6 miles. Turn right onto Ford Pkwy., and in 0.8 mile turn left onto 46th Ave. S. Immediately turn left onto Godfrey Pkwy., and parking will be on the right.

This three-trail network offers a variety of multiuse opportunities between the cities of Duluth and Hinckley: the Alex Laveau Memorial Trail, the Matthew Lourey State Trail, and the Hinckley-Duluth segment of the Willard Munger State Trail. Together they offer several connecting routes through this area of Minnesota just beyond the western edge of Lake Superior. The Munger and Laveau Trails meet in the town of Carlton. Lying east of these two trails is the Matthew Lourey State Trail, known locally as the Boundary segment of this trail system.

Biking, hiking, and in-line skating are popular summer activities along the 160-mile trail. Winter activity

The southern portion of the trail offers open views, rural landscapes, and rustic towns.

Location
Carlton, Pine

Endpoints
Second St. N.W./County Road 18 and Old Highway 61 N. (Hinckley) to Pulaski St. and Bayhill Drive (Duluth)

Mileage
160

Type
Rail-Trail

Roughness Index
1

Surface
Asphalt

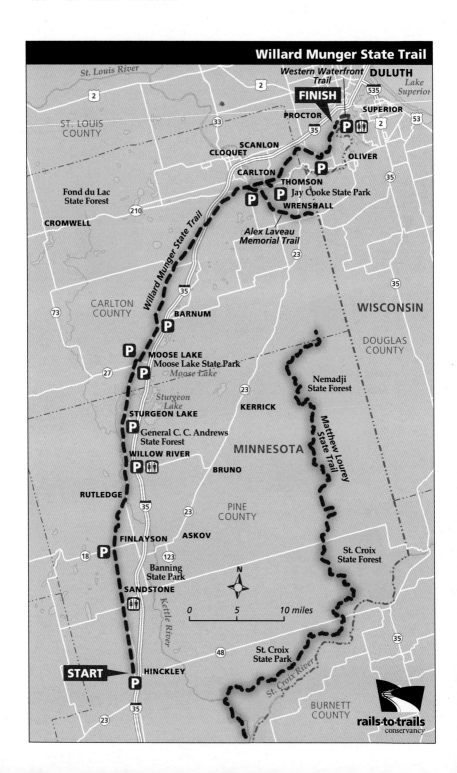

Willard Munger State Trail

along the trail includes snowmobiling and cross-country skiing. This trail system winds its way through striking forested landscapes along a railroad route that played a life-saving role during the Hinckley/Cloquet fires that ravaged this area in the early 1900s.

The Hinckley-Duluth segment of the Willard Munger State Trail stretches more than 60 miles between central Minnesota and the state's gateway to Lake Superior. This section of the trail follows the historic 19th-century route of the Lake Superior & Mississippi Railroad that carried goods and passengers between the Twin Cities and Duluth. Because it is completely paved and relatively flat, the pathway is perfect for bikers, walkers, and in-line skaters during warmer months and snowmobilers and cross-country skiers in the winter. Along the way, trail users will enjoy stunning natural scenery, especially the northernmost 15-mile section between Carlton and Duluth. Here, you will travel through rocky cliffs and over the St. Louis River Gorge.

The trail skirts the northern edge of the Jay Cooke State Park, which, with its pristine forests, waterfalls, and swinging suspension bridge, is definitely worth a stop. The southern portion of the trail (Carlton to Hinckley) offers open views, rural landscapes, and rustic towns. River crossings, lakes, and ponds add to the picturesque backdrop. Shortly before passing the town of Willow River, you'll travel through the gently rolling terrain of General C. C. Andrews State Forest, a beautiful respite with its tall stands of pine, birch, aspen, and oak trees.

The Alex Laveau Memorial Trail is a 16-mile spur heading south from the city of Carlton that connects the suburban section of Gary-New Duluth in southwestern Duluth. The 6-mile section of trail between Carlton and MN 23, just past Wrenshall, is an off-road paved trail. The remaining 10 miles is routed along paved county roads and city streets. At the northern end of the Alex Laveau Memorial Trail is a seamless connection to the Western Waterfront Trail, offering 5 more miles of scenic waterfront trail.

The Matthew Lourey State Trail is an 80-mile natural-surface trail used primarily for horseback riding, hiking, mountain biking, and snowmobiling. It represents a backcountry setting through remote sections of Minnesota state forests. Some sections of the trail can be impassable in the summer.

Bicycle tune-up stations have been installed in the trailhead parking lots in Hinckley, Moose Lake, and Carlton, and near the park office in Jay Cooke State Park.

CONTACT: dnr.state.mn.us/state_trails/willard_munger

DIRECTIONS

Parking is available at the southern trailhead in Hinckley, one block north of the Hinckley Fire Museum, at the intersection of Old US 61 and County Road 18. Take I-35 to Exit 180. Head southwest on MN 23, and go 0.2 mile. Turn right onto CR 61, and go 3.1 miles. Turn left onto Second St. N.W., and parking will be on the right in 0.1 mile.

At the northern trailhead in Duluth, parking is available just south of the Lake Superior Zoo at the intersection of Grand Ave. and 75th Ave. W. Take I-35 N. to Exit 251A. Merge onto Cody St., and in 0.2 mile turn right onto N. 63rd Ave. W. In 0.6 mile take a slight right onto MN 23/Grand Ave., and go 1 mile. Parking will be on the right.

Parking is also available in Jay Cooke State Park, in Moose Lake State Park, and at the Hemlock Ravine Scientific and Natural Area on CR 151 just north of its intersection with MN 210.

The Mesabi Trail travels through a region known for its large deposits of iron ore (see page 101).

Index

A

Afton to Lakeland Trail, 8–10
Aitkin City Park, 41
Albert Lea, Albert Lea Lake, 17, 19
Alex Laveau Memorial Trail, 149
Anderson Park, Red Wing, 31

B

"Ballad of Casey Jones," 33
Bassett Creek Regional Trail, 117
Beaver Island Trail, 11–13
bicycling, 4–5
Big Rivers Regional Trail, 14–16
Big Tooth Ridge Park, 69
Blazing Star State Trail, 17–19
Blue Earth River, 133
Blue Ox Trail, 121
book, how to use this, 3–5
Bottineau, Pierre, 21
Bottineau Trail, 7, 20–22
Brackett Field Park, Minneapolis, 106
Brown's Creek Nature Preserve, 25
Brown's Creek State Trail, 23–25, 58
Bruce Vento Regional Trail, 26–28, 58
Bryn Mawr Meadows Park, 118
Burlington Northern Railroad, 39, 63, 77, 95, 119, 141

C

Cannon Falls, 29, 31
Cannon Lake, 133
Cannon River, 29
Cannon Valley Trail, 29–31, 67
Carver Park Reserve, 94
Casey Jones State Trail, 32–34
Cass Lake, 85
Cedar Lake, 118
Cedar Lake LRT Regional Trail, 35–37, 117, 118

Central Lakes State Trail, 38–40
Chain of Lakes, 105
Chautauqua Lake, 40
Chicago Great Western Railway, 29, 53, 65
Chippewa National Forest, 83
Clearwater River, 21
Coldspring, 127
Cold Spring, 125
Cold Spring Baseball Park, 127
Covered Bridge Park, Zumbrota, 67
Crocker Park, Lakeland, 9
Crow Wing State Park, 119, 121
Cuyuna Country State Recreation Area, 41
Cuyuna Lakes State Trail, 41–43

D

Dairyland Trail, 44–46
Dakota Indian tribe, 121
Dakota Indian tribe, Great Sioux Nation, 119, 131
Dakota Rail corridor, 47
Dakota Rail Regional Trail, 47–49
Delagoon Park, 39
descriptions, trail, 3–4
detailed trail maps, 3
Dinkytown Greenway, 50–52, 139, 147
dogs, 5
Douglas State Trail, 53–55
Duluth, Red Wing & Southern Railroad, 65

E

Eagle Lake, 133
Eastside Heritage Park, Saint Paul, 28
Electric Short Line Railroad, 99
Elgin, 71, 73
Elk River, 69, 72
etiquette, trail, 4–5
Excelsior Amusement Park, 94
Eyota, 71

F

Father Hennepin Bluff Park, 139
featured trails, 8–152
Fergus Falls, Otter Tail County, 39, 97
First Bridge Park, Minneapolis, 139
Forest History Center, Grand Rapids, 103
Forest Lake, 79, 142
Fort Snelling, 15, 112
Fort Snelling State Park, 107, 109
Frank Hall Park, Albert Lea, 17

G

Gateway State Trail, 23, 28, 56–58
General C. C. Andrews State Forest, 151
Gitchi-Gami State Trail, 59–61, 145
Glacial Gardens of Interstate State Park, 89

Glacial Lakes State Trail, 62–64, 125
Goodhue Pioneer State Trail, 31, 65–67
Gooseberry Falls State Park, 61
Grand Marais Corridor Trail, 61
Grand Rounds Scenic Byway System, 107, 148
Great Northern Railroad, 69, 137
Great Northern Trail, 68–70
Great River Ridge State Trail, viii, 71–73
Greenway of Greater Grand Forks, 74–76

H

Hardwood Creek Regional Trail, 77–79, 141, 142
Harmony, 81, 82
Harmony–Preston Valley State Trail, 80–82, 130

The Midtown Greenway is one of two trails in Minnesota that has been inducted into the Rail-Trail Hall of Fame (see page 104).

H *(continued)*

Hay Creek Valley Campground, 67
Heartland State Trail, 83–85, 121
Hennepin County Regional Railroad
   Authority (HCRRA), 37
Heritage Trail, 1, 139
Hiawatha Trail, 86–88
Hill, James J., 137
Hinckley-Duluth segment, Willard
   Munger State Trail, 149, 151
Holdingford, 95, 97
how to use this book, 3–5
Hugo, 77

I

icons
   map, 3
   trail use, 5
Interstate State Park to Taylors Falls Trail,
   89–91
Iron Range region, 101

J

James E. Rice Park, 148
Jay Cooke State Park, 145, 151
Jones, Casey, 33

Dinkytown Greenway opened in 2013 (see page 50).

K

Kaposia Park, Minneapolis, 115
Keillor, Garrison, 95
Kenilworth Trail, 35, 117, 118
Kensington Runestone, 40

L

Lake Bemidji State Park, 121
Lake Elysian, 133
Lake Koronis, 64
Lake Koronis Recreational Trail, 127
Lakeland Trail, from Afton, 8–10
Lake Louise State Park, 135, 136
Lake Minnetonka, 47, 94
Lake Minnetonka LRT Regional Trail, 92–94
Lake Phalen trail, 28
Lake Shetek State Park, 34
Lakeside Park, 79
Lake Superior, 59, 143
Lake Superior & Mississippi Railroad, 151
Lake Waconia, 49
Lake Wilson, 34
Lake Wobegon Trail, 2, 40, 45, 95–97
Laura Ingalls Wilder museum, Walnut Grove, 34
Leech Lake, 85
Le Sueur River, 1
Luce Line Trail, 98–100, 118

M

map icons, 3
maps
    See also specific trail
    Minnesota, 6
    state locator, detailed trail, 3
Martin Olav Sabo Bridge, Minneapolis, 106
Matthew Lourey State Trail, 149, 151
McKinley Park, St. Cloud, 13
Medicine Lake, 99

Meier, Margie, 136
Memorial Park, Shakopee, 111
Mendota, 15
Mesabi Iron Range, 1
Mesabi Trail, 101–103
Metrodome, Minneapolis, 87, 88
Midtown Greenway, 104–106, 147
Milwaukee Road, 123
Minneapolis, iv, 1, 11, 35–37, 50–52, 86–88, 98–100, 104–106, 107–109, 116–118, 137–139, 146–148
Minneapolis and Northwestern Railway Company, 11
Minneapolis and St. Louis Railway, 37, 99
Minneapolis Commercial Railway, 105
Minnehaha Creek, Minnehaha Park, 87, 88
Minnehaha Falls, 107, 109
Minnehaha Regional Park, 106, 107, 109, 147
Minnehaha Trail, 107–109
Minneopa State Park, 124
Minnesota
    introduction to, 1
    map, 6
Minnesota Central Railroad, 15
Minnesota River, 15, 111, 112, 123
Minnesota River Bluffs LRT Regional Trail, 117
Minnesota Twins, 118
Minnesota Valley State Recreation Area, 112
Minnesota Valley State Trail, 110–112
Minnesota Western, 99
Minnetonka, 94
Mississippi National River and Recreation Area, 16, 113
Mississippi River, 11, 15, 51, 105, 106, 107, 109, 115, 118, 137, 148
Mississippi River Gorge Regional Trail, 147

M *(continued)*

Mississippi River Regional Trail (Dakota County), 113–115
Morgan Park, 145
Mower County Natural & Scenic Area, 135
Myre–Big Island State Park, 17

N

Nicollet Island, 139
North Cedar Lake Regional Trail, 35, 36, 106, 116–118
Northern Pacific Railway, 51
North Minnesota River Trail, 123, 133
Northshore Mining Railroad, 61

O

Ojibwe Indian tribe, 119, 121
O'Leary Park, 76

P

parking (map icon), 3
Paul Bunyan State Forest, 83
Paul Bunyan State Trail, 1, 119–121
Phalen-Keller Regional Park, 58
photo credits, 164
Pine Bend Bluff Scientific & Natural Area, 115
Pine Island trailhead, 55
Pine Point Regional Park, 57, 58
Pipestone National Monument, 34
Plainview, 71
Prairie Home Companion, A (Keillor), 95
Preston, 82

R

Rails-to-Trails Conservancy (RTC), iii, 151, 165

rail-trails
    described, 1–2
    trail use, 4–5
rail-with-trails, 2
Rapidan Dam Park, 124
Red Jacket, 123
Red Jacket Trail, 1, 122–124
Red Jacket Trestle, 1, 123
Red Lake Falls, 21
Red Lake River, 21, 22, 75, 76
Red River, 75, 76
Red River State Recreation Area, 76
Red Wing, 29
restroom (map icon), 3
Richard J. Dorer Memorial Hardwood State Forest, 65
Rochester, 53, 55
Rockville granite quarry, 127
Rocori Trail, 64, 125–127
Root River, 82
Root River State Trail, x, 81, 82, 128–130
Root River/Harmony–Preston Valley trail network, 130
Rural Bicycle Loop, Grand Forks, ND, 75

S

safety guidelines, 4–5
Saint Paul, 57
Sakatah Lake, 133
Sakatah Lake State Park, 133
Sakatah Singing Hills State Trail, 31, 123, 131–133
Sauk River, 127
Scenic River Trail, 13
Seventh Street Improvement Arches, Saint Paul, 27
Shooting Star Prairie Scientific & Natural Area, 135
Shooting Star State Trail, 134–136
Sibley Historic Site, 16

Sibley State Park, 64
Silver Creek Cliff, 59, 61
Simon's Ravine, 113
Snelling State Park Bottomlands Trail, 16
Soo Line Railroad, 45, 58
Soo Line Recreational Trail, 97
South Route Trail, 124
Split Rock Lighthouse State Park, 61
Spring Lake Park Reserve, 113, 115
St. Anthony Falls, 1, 52
St. Anthony Falls Heritage Trail, 137–139,
   147
state locator maps, 3
St. Cloud State University, 11
St. Croix River, 9, 23, 89
Stillwater, 23

St. John's University, 97
St. Louis River, 143
Stone Arch Bridge, 1, 52, 137, 139
Sunrise Prairie Trail, 79, 140–142
Sunrise River, 141, 142
Superior Hiking Trail, 145
Swede Hollow Park, Saint Paul, 28
Swedish Immigrant Trail State Project,
   91

T

Target Field, 118
Taylors Falls Trail, from Interstate State
   Park, 89–91
TCF Bank Stadium, 51

The Paul Bunyan State Trail became part of the Rail-Trail Hall of Fame in 2011 (see page 119).

T *(continued)*

Temperance River, 61
Theodore Wirth Regional Park, 99, 100, 117
Three Rivers Park District trail system, 99
Tileston, 11
Top of the World Park, 69
trail descriptions, 3–4
trail etiquette, 4–5
trail use icons, 5
TrailLink.com trail-finder website, iii, 4–5
trails, 6
  featured, 8–152
  keys to trail use, 5
  rail-trails, 1–2
  trail maps, 3
  use, 4–5
Two Harbors, 59, 61

U

United States Hockey Hall of Fame Museum, Eveleth, 103
University of Minnesota campus, 51, 139, 147

V

Vento, Bruce Frank, 27
Victoria, 93–94

W

Walker, 85
Warren pony truss bridge, Red Lake Falls, 22
Wells Lake, 133
Western Waterfront Trail (WWT), 143–145, 151
West River Parkway, 117
West River Parkway Trail, iv, 52, 139, 146–148
Wheel Passes, 31
White Bear Lake, 28
Whitewater River, North Fork, 73
Whitewater State Park, 73
Wilder, Laura Ingalls, 34
Willard Munger State Trail system, 23, 143, 149–152
William O'Brien State Park, 58
Willmar Civic Center trailhead bike repair station unit, 63
Winchell Trail, 148
Woodland Trails Park, 72
Wynne Lake, 101

Z

Zumbro River, 53

Opposite: *Cyclists of all skill levels enjoy the Root River State Trail (see page 128).*

Photo Credits

Support Rails-to-Trails Conservancy

The nation's leader in helping communities transform unused rail lines and connecting corridors into multiuse trails, Rails-to-Trails Conservancy (RTC) depends on the support of its members and donors to create access to healthy outdoor experiences.

Your donation will help support programs and services that have helped put more than 22,000 rail-trail miles on the ground. Every day, RTC provides vital assistance to communities to develop and maintain trails throughout the country. In addition, RTC advocates for trail-friendly policies, promotes the benefits of rail-trails, and defends rail-trail laws in the courts.

Join online at **railstotrails.org,** or mail your donation to Rails-to-Trails Conservancy, 2121 Ward Court N.W., Fifth Floor, Washington, D.C. 20037.

Rails-to-Trails Conservancy is a 501(c)(3) nonprofit organization, and contributions are tax deductible.

Presented by

rails·to·trails
conservancy

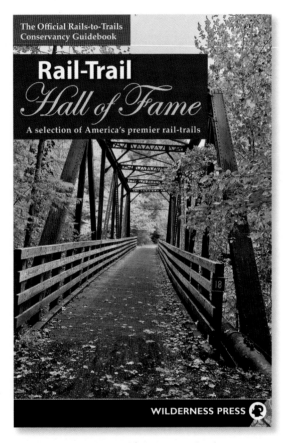

Rail-Trail Hall of Fame

ISBN: 978-0-89997-825-3
$16.95, 1st Edition

152 pages, full-color
maps and photos

Explore premier rail-trails across America with this official guide. In 2007 Rails-to-Trails Conservancy began recognizing exemplary rail-trails through its Rail-Trail Hall of Fame.

These Hall of Fame rail-trails are found in 28 states and in nearly every environment—from downtown urban corridors to pathways stretching across wide-open prairie, along coastlines, or through mountain ranges.